ANGELA GILES AND GALIT VENTURA-ROZEN
WITH 49 AMAZING WOMEN

Everyday woman's

Guide To Doing What You Love

51 Stories From Purpose Driven Women

Contents

Introduction

During one of the most challenging times of most of our lives, the pandemic of 2020, something beautiful was born Everyday Woman. Why? The world shutdown and we saw an immediate need for women to learn how to take their business online and make money. We started a FB group, women supporting women professionals and entrepreneurs and immediately started providing complimentary videos and workshops for women to learn how to get more clients and be more visible. As of the time of this book being published, we are over 12,000 members and growing steadily every day.

We have covered everything from social media platforms, to becoming an author, to getting to 7 figures in your business and more. We started a community that would give women a place to feel supported and uplifted when it was necessary for their success but also including the logical tools to be successful online and in their business.

We both have successful businesses online and off and realized that we must step up and share our own methods to success to support other women from all over the world. Everyday Woman has reached just about every country, nationality, culture, religion and age. There is one main thing in common that the

Everyday Woman has, it is *women supporting women* as the foundation for every single member of the group.

Our mission from day one was You + Me = Community. It takes a village of women to support each other and believe in each other to have the success you want and we are aware of that and want to continue to believe in that mission.

How can you be a part of this mission? Look for ways to support other women that can learn from you, that may have challenges in their business or profession and recognize there is enough success to go around for all of us.

Our challenge to you is to be the change you want to see in the world and know without a doubt we are better together.

Xoxo

Galit & Angela

Co – Founders of Everyday Woman

www.everydaywoman.me

Galit Ventura-Rozen

Co Founder of Everyday Woman

Sales Success Expert

https://www.everydaywoman.me

https://www.salessuccessexpert.com

https://www.linkedin.com/in/galitventurarozen

https://www.instagram.com/galitventurarozen

https://www.facebook.com/galitventurarozen

As a sales success expert and award-winning entrepreneur, Galit Ventura-Rozen began her journey into entrepreneurship as a commercial real estate broker over 25 years ago. She now owns and operates Commercial Professionals, a $1 billion dollar company She has made it her mission to show women how to reach 7+ figures in their business through sales success. Her goal is to empower, inspire, and motivate others to believe in themselves incorporating lessons from her book, The Successful Woman's Mindset.

Galit also created Empowering University which offers corporate training, workshops, retreats, and professional speaking. Galit is co-founder of the Everyday Woman's movement to build a community where women receive support and are uplifted to do and be what they desire in their life and business.

She has also been featured in P.O.W.E.R. Magazine, Wealthy Woman Magazine, and on the cover of the Top 100 Real Estate Agent's Magazine. As a sought-after internationally recognized public speaker, Galit has appeared on ABC, NBC, and Fox as an expert on mindset, leadership, and business.

She has received many awards over the years, most recently Silver State Awards Entrepreneur of the Year and Women of distinction award for Professional Services.

Chapter 1

Women Empowering Women

By Galit Ventura-Rozen

My first memory of empowering a woman was when I was in high school trying out for cheerleading. I was trying out for cheerleading and a past cheerleader that had to try out again was overcome with fear that she wouldn't make it again. We did not run in the same circles or really know each other, but I looked at her and said, "You can do this, I believe in you." She made it on the team and I didn't. I really can't recall the two of us really speaking again after that. For me that started my journey of recognizing that sometimes even a few words of support or even a smile, may make a difference in another woman's life.

It's quite ironic that today I am co-founder of a group with over 11,000 women that is growing daily, that I get up on stage and speak each year in front of 1000's of women, that I have been on television numerous times and I am interviewed regularly on podcasts. Why is it ironic? Because I have 3 younger brothers and most of my close friends growing up were boys. I think I never felt like I belonged in a specific group of girls when I was younger and today, I still struggle to feel like I belong in different women's groups.

Don't mistake this to think I don't keep networking, meeting new women every day and empowering and inspiring them as much as I can. If you asked me why I feel like the outcast often, I probably would respond and say I am truly an introvert at heart.

I love working with women, I love inspiring and empowering women and I love showing women how to be more visible, get more clients and build their own dreams/business to 7 figures. I truly love that. Is it easy for me to be so public, interviewed, speak on stage and train employees at companies? Not always, but that does not mean I should stop doing it.

For me doing what you love and empowering women isn't about you, it's about the one woman that makes a different decision today that can change her life and bring happiness to her. That is what drives me. That is my purpose and passion and that is what EVERYDAY WOMAN is built on.

How can you start empowering women today? Keep your eyes open on social media and at networking events for the one woman that may be standing in a corner alone, or that one woman that is dealing with a challenge today and posts about it. Offer your support, tell that woman you believe in her and watch a world open up that involves beautiful things for you and for anyone you choose to empower with your gifts, your kindness and your love.

Angela Giles

Co Founder of Everyday Woman

Marketing Expert

https://www.everydaywoman.me

https://www.angelagiles.com

https://www.linkedin.com/in/angelakaygiles

https://www.instagram.com/angelaksgiles

https://www.facebook.com/angelakgiles

Angela Giles is a self-made businesswoman, author, speaker, and consultant leading people to their path to success. She is one of the most sought-after business coaches for lead generation on the West Coast.

Angela offers her clients a dynamic program that is based on simple secrets for BIG results. She is committed to helping independent entrepreneurs, business owners and professionals accelerate their business profits and increase their bottom line. Since launching the Simple Profit Method, she has helped her clients to achieve 6-figure launches and go from making mediocre sales to effortlessly generating thousands of dollars in a few short weeks.

Angela has a solid 18-yearbackground with proven performance in business consulting and marketing. She also holds a bachelor's degree in political science. It is this combination that has helped to develop her entirely unique and highly successful approach to analyzing consumer behavior and staying on top of an ever-changing industry.

She is a regular speaker on the topic of influential communication and marketing and her book *From Mind to Mouth* walks readers through the essentials of communicating effectively with anybody, anywhere— as this is the key (and often missing) ingredient when it comes to closing a sale.

Angela lives in Henderson with her husband Allen, their three teenage boys (who always keep her on her toes) and three dogs: Pixie, Wishbone and Maddie. She's an avid reader and has a genuine love for connecting with people. Her favorite pastime is spending time with other women empowering them to reach their highest potential. She does this by volunteering and serving on the local board of Women of Global Change. Whenever she's not working or sleeping, she is in passionate pursuit of those who want the satisfaction of leading happy, successful and productive lives.

Chapter 2

Time is Your New Currency

By Angela Giles

Most of my life, I was taught that if I worked hard, I would have success. In fact, I think most of my generation was taught that concept. Your output was a measurement of your success.

With this framework, everything I did was based around money as my currency. When I decided I wanted to do something, I thought about how much money I could receive from it. Pleasure was a secondary thing.

It really didn't matter honestly if I liked the "thing" or not. I would do it if it could bring me money.

Fast forward twenty years into my life, I realized that some of the things that I worked so hard to get, I no longer valued. For example, was that old dusty $3500 vacuum in my closet something I even used?

NO!

Was that latest kitchen gadget I bought in the middle of the night something I even used?

NO!.

It is when I had that ah ha moment that I had life all backwards.

I could never get back my time that I spent earning money to buy things that I no longer needed.

What if instead, I measured my currency in terms of time. It would change how I looked at everything.

It also made me realize that I didn't have to do everything. The first step was when I wanted to purchase either an item or an experience, I would factor out how much time it would take for me to get that thing.

Then, the next step I would do if I thought that the time wasn't worth it, I would sit and think if there was a way for me to hand that time off, to someone else to do the work and get the thing I wanted. You know, the concept of outsourcing.

When I used this "new" principle of time as my new currency I found that I had more time, more experiences & seemed to be able to afford the finer things in life.

It became my passion to share with others how to do this to have a more meaningful life, by treating time as their currency instead of money.

Hanna Olivas

Author, Speaker and Transformational Coach

Co-Founder She Rises Studios

https://www.sherisesstudios.com

https://www.bbbcf.org

https://www.linkedin.com//in/sherisesstudios

https://www.instagram.com/sherisesstudios

https://www.facebook.com/sherisesstudios

Hanna Olivas is a wife , mother, and grandmother.

She was born and raised in Las Vegas , Nevada.

A journeyman makeup artist for over 20 years.

She is the founder of The Brave and Beautiful Blood Cancer Foundation and the Co-founder of She Rises Studios. She is a Best Selling author, and Motivational speaker. She travels the world sharing her journey and empowering women globally.

Chapter 3

Becoming an Unstoppable Woman

By Hanna Olivas

After being diagnosed with terminal cancer, I had to completely change my life, mindset, my entire world. I needed to find balance, peace and learn to accept the diagnosis and continue to do what I love every day. Despite my symptoms and how I feel physically and emotionally. I wanted to "Become An Unstoppable Woman"!

I am a wife, mother, grandmother, daughter, sister and friend. I run four successful businesses including a local nonprofit for blood cancer patients, as well as co-founder of She Rises Studios.

After the news I received I made up my mind that NOTHING would change that. I began to learn, shift and have the willingness to grow into a new mindset and lifestyle.

Becoming Unstoppable meant I had to persevere and believe in myself despite any circumstances. The process is not overnight, it's building your resilience and determination muscle, but also living in gratitude all the time.

I have to be intentional from the time I rise till the time I sleep. I have to stay focused. I rise daily with the expectation of abundance, love, peace, health, amazing relationships and a zealous will for life. I never take one day for granted or the people in it. Many have asked me "How Do I Live knowing I am terminally Ill"?

My answer is "I am Dying to Live, Not Living to Die".

As women we face many adversities, struggles, heartache, loss, depression, health issues, financial ruin and more. It's how we handle some of these inevitable issues that matters.

"Becoming an Unstoppable Woman" isn't just for the women entrepreneurs. It's for the stay at home mom, the single mother, college student, teenage girl, wife, grandmother. It's for the Everyday Women!

So, build your mindset, tenacity and perseverance muscles. Break Through Before You Break Down. Begin and end your days knowing and believing you are Unstoppable.

You are authentically and beautifully you.

Rise Up, Lead, Live and Enjoy being the Everyday, Unstoppable Woman, that I know you can be and are already!

I strongly encourage you to find a mentor, or coach to help you develop your skills, muscle and strength in this journey. Wake up early. Set goals, stay on task. Read books that fill your mind with positive and creative value. Get organized.

Write down on paper what you want your life to look like. Design it and live it. Does this all sound scary to you? Maybe a little overwhelming? It's not I promise.

To the Everyday Woman,

I hope you find your passion, your purpose, your perseverance, strength and tenacity to live Everyday boldly with expectations of abundance, love and excellent health.

Dawn Britt

CEO/ Founder

OneSeven Agency

https://www.onesevenagency.com

https://www.linkedin.com/in/dawnbritt

https://www.instagram.com/princessbritt17

https://www.facebook.com/dprincessbritt

Dawn Britt

"In order to be irreplaceable, one must always be different."

- Coco Chanel

With a hands-on approach to doing business, Dawn Britt oversees client strategy and crisis communications while empowering and developing a strong team of practitioners within OneSeven Agency. Her refreshingly sincere, straightforward approach has resulted in affiliations with countless well-known industry movers and shakers, along with meaningful partnerships and placements for her clients.

With more than 20 years in the PR and marketing game, Britt helms a dynamic agency, providing a diverse set of clientele with innovative representation. Throughout her career, she's worked with a who's who of distinguished brands and non-profits.

Britt was the Executive Corporate Director of Communications for Fortune 100 Sands Corp., where she was a driving force behind the $1.9 billion Palazzo grand opening. She created OneSeven Agency to provide clients with what she sought while in-house, giving her an innate ability to both process and produce visionary service for her client's goals. Always looking ahead to "what's next," Britt's digital team was one of the first to incorporate digital influencers in measurable contracted campaigns in the Las Vegas market.

Named PRSA's "PR Practitioner of the Year," Britt has lectured to UNLV's Journalism and Media Studies program, served as President-Elect for the PRSA Las Vegas Valley Chapter and was an advocate at the Global Gaming Expo. She is currently a board member for the Las Vegas Chapter of Dress For Success, she served two years as a board member and marketing chair for the Las Vegas Fashion Council and is actively involved in fundraising support and volunteering efforts for numerous charities and is part of the Las Vegas Chamber Leadership Class of 2021.

Britt spends quality time with her fiance and business partner, H Farahi, and their shih tzu, MeiLi, while touring vineyards, hosting parties, practicing pilates, traveling and hitting the dining scene.

Chapter 4

Get to it: Starting your own business

By Dawn Britt

Becoming an entrepreneur may not be easy but it is exciting. How do you leave that corporate world to do what you love and what you are truly passionate about? Especially when you have security meaning a steady paycheck, benefits and structure.

I was putting in tremendous hours and efforts working for someone else, so I thought, why not do the same but for myself. After 12 years working for a Fortune 100 company as an executive overseeing communications and marketing, earning a nice steady income, yearly bonuses, excellent health benefits and working with an incredible team and a big budget, I decided to break free and open my own PR/marketing company. I decided it was time to take the plunge and give it my all.

In my case, I was doing what I loved to do but I was doing for someone else and putting in many long hours. I gave myself a one year deadline to develop my business, working early mornings or late at night, whenever I could be researching everything and creating my business plan. I talked to friends and colleagues about what I was planning to do. While doing such, I had learned that a close colleague was getting ready to open a restaurant in Napa Valley and he asked me if I would be interested in helping him launch it. Shortly after, I had another colleague whom I worked with in the past ask me if I could take them on. I had two clients ready to jump on board as soon as I was ready! I didn't need much money to start my business other than a website, business cards, cell phone, internet, laptop and my network.

Tips and things I have learned:

- Just do it. Don't be afraid,

- When determining what type of business, you want to start looking for a gap in the market and think about what you can do to fill that niche.

- It is important to learn about the financial and legal side of running a business and hire experts in that area.

- Focus, build and maintain relationships with EVERYONE. You never know when a relationship will become an opportunity.

- Don't just rely on referrals to grow your business. Have a business development plan in place and be consistent about implementing it.

- Don't open a business if you think you are going to make a ton of money and will have a steady paycheck. Right from the start any money earned should go back into the business.

- Those 60+ hours I was working at my other job? Yes, that became double with my business. I actually never stop working.

- Read multiple digital subscriptions and newsletters within your industry.

- There may not be much money in the beginning to hire full-time employees so develop an intern program.

- Look for veterans in your industry or other businesses offering services that complement yours, meet with them and discuss a possible strategic partnership.

  Now get to it!

Darla Makela

Darla Makela Coaching

Owner & CEO, Visionary Leader

https://www.darlamakela.com

https://www.linkedin.com/in/darla-makela-72500714

https://www.instagram.com/darlamakelacoaching

https://www.facebook.com/darla.makela

Darla Makela has lived a life of service supporting and inspiring women through years of non-profit opportunities. She was also a leader in Corporate America for 27 years. She is a Certified Life and Health Coach and Master Mindset Coach who is passionate about helping women change their mind so they can change their life.

She is a Visionary leader that is committed to helping powerful Women create a life-changing vision. This includes providing the tools and support that they need to make that vision come to life, whether that be at home, in the workplace, in ministry or as an entrepreneur.

Darla is available for 1 on 1 coaching, small group coaching, workshops and retreats. All of which are focused on equipping and inspiring women to listen, dream, take action and become all that they were created to be!

Chapter 5

Change Your Mind. Change Your Life.

By Darla Makela

As a young girl I remember many times where I received messages (or at least experienced things that caused me to believe) that I was not good enough in so many ways.

Little would I know that well into my adulthood I would be haunted by those beliefs that had become deeply ingrained in my heart and all-consuming in my mind.

As I began to recognize that my life could be different, I began to long for the day where I would feel peace instead of conflict. Where joy would replace anxiety. Where confidence would defeat all of the limiting thoughts that I was believing.

Well, my passionate and intentional searching led me to many resources that would eventually provide what I needed to become the powerful woman that I am today and I want to share my most impactful tool with you.

I say it is my life motto because it says SO many things!

"Your thoughts create your feelings. Your feelings create your actions. Your actions create your results."

Simple enough but very powerful. I encourage you to take a few minutes and read that until it really makes sense to you.

From this we can see that it all begins with the thoughts that we allow ourselves to entertain and join forces with.

I am sure that if you think about it you can recall a time (or more) where you literally felt your body changing as you were mulling over a situation, belief, or message that was given to you.

As your body began to react to your thoughts, do you recall the actions that you began to take, possibly without even knowing exactly what you were doing?

Then, the results…sadness, stress, broken relationships…just a few of the potential outcomes you may have experienced.

Today, however, I want you to know that it does not have to be this way for you! Just like my life has been transformed by changing my mind, so can yours!

First, you must take those thoughts captive and replace them with a greater truth or belief! Take note, it may take you a while to actually **believe** what you **know** to be true.

Second, practice gratitude every single day! Where there is gratitude the negative cannot survive.

Third, be consistent. Just like any new habit that you take on, this will also take time. I promise you that if you commit to taking your thoughts captive, practicing gratitude and being consistent in these things your life will truly be changed!

Since I have committed to these great practices, I have seen amazing things happen in my life and my career!

I am attracting the perfect clients. I have powerful relationships and I have seen incredible growth in everything I do.

Because of this I am able to impact people all around me in my daily life which allows them to impact their world as they, too, live out their personally designed life purpose!

Liza Rogers

Founder, Dreamer, Action Taker

WREN - Women's Real Estate Network

https://www.lizarogers.com

https://wren.club

https://www.linkedin.com/in/lizarogers

https://www.instagram.com/wrenclub

https://www.facebook.com/wren4us

Liza Rogers

For 25 years Liza has been passionately involved in what is now being called "the cohousing movement". Liza's deep and diverse background in tourism and events has included leading groups on world-famous European river cruises, managing Eco guesthouses in Bondi Beach Australia, and being employed by two Olympic Games.

On her journey she discovered everything about financing, joint ventures, and buying real estate. Liza has a wealth of information and wisdom about real estate sectors both inside and outside Canadian borders.

As the Founder and Leader of WREN, Liza feels compelled to provide opportunities for others, especially women, to find their own creative and collaborative ways to learn about and prosper from real estate and related markets. She is currently in the process of purchasing a portfolio of investment properties with a group of women and has just partnered on the purchase 150 acres of subdividable land near Victoria, BC.

Chapter 6

Collaborating for the WIN

By Liza Rogers

I've always sought adventure, the traditional roles of mom, wife, career woman never called to me. I'm 51 and I've stayed single and without kids by design, my design. I was conceived in Canada, born in England, moved back to Canada at three and have moved about 60 times. Sometimes from one street to another, other times from one country to another and occasionally from one ship to another. My life is extraordinary and I'm honored to be creating my own path and sharing it with others. Care to join me?

As the Founder and Leader of the Women's Real Estate Network (WREN), I'm passionate about providing opportunities for women to find their own creative and collaborative ways to learn about and prosper from real estate and related markets. Personally, I'm building a portfolio of investment properties with a group of women including very recently a new 150-acre subdivision near Victoria, BC.

I'm not driven by money, however I *am* driven by the freedom money buys. When I look at what Real Estate offers, it seems to provide me with the best possible vehicle to create the life of my dreams.

When I turned forty, I realized that with the type of work I had chosen and the type of nomadic lifestyle I wanted to continue to live (and was currently leading), I would never be able to retire on that income alone.

So, I explored. What could I do that could ensure wealth, community, freedom and income.? The ONLY answer I found was Real Estate.

Real Estate is one of the most secure and valuable investments you can make and it's possible to borrow up to 95% of the funds required to purchase a property!

My lessons began. I researched and took advantage of as many free or inexpensive Real Estate education seminars as I could find learning about cash flow, access to credit, risk tolerance, joint ventures, student housing and more.

I also realized that women weren't investing even though they drive the real estate market! For women in particular, collaboration is key. Share the risk and the reward so you can also feel good about building wealth alongside each other. Find your tribe! and for goodness sakes GET IN THE GAME!

I met many women like me and we would explore our mutual goals over coffee, then coffee became wine and wine became full days of running and crunching numbers, looking at properties and finding the team and so, WREN was born. Although it was all very exciting, I can tell you, none of it was easy when I first got started!

We started with a half-duplex for $495,000 and sold it three years later for $720,000. Excellent, right?

We learned about pumps and toilets and in-floor heating. We learned about separating the business, the house and the personalities. We learned about finding the right realtor for the purchase AND for the sale. We learned about crunching the numbers over and over again.

If you're thinking that you'd like some wealth, freedom and a collaborative tribe think about investing in Real Estate, with women.

Lollo Molander

Creative Strategist

Boundless Brilliance AB

https://www.boundlessbrilliance.com

https://www.linkedin.com/in/liselottemolander

https://www.instagram.com/lollomolander

https://www.facebook.com/lollomolander

I'm Lollo Molander, an executive creative strategist and speaker that help hustling entrepreneurs achieve Boundless Brilliance to excel in life and business.

For over 20 years, I've been supporting leaders and their teams to take full responsibility for their life and goals and equip them with the right tools to achieve those outcomes in half the time and without burnout.

When executives and entrepreneurs want to become the version of themselves that can surpass every milestone and live a life so abundant that no one in their family has ever created, they seek my guidance.

Boundless Brilliance helps them to do the internal work required to make decisions as their next-level multimillion version and not from their current hustling and overworked self.

My clients have achieved extraordinary results in their personal and professional life. Yet, they are not satisfied and envision creating a dynastic legacy that lasts for generations to come.

Chapter 7

From Burnout to Bliss

By Lollo Molander

I grew up in the south of Sweden. My childhood memories are all about climbing trees and playing in the forest. I was creative and my parents were allowing and supportive of my various expressions.

My interest was in teaching and textiles and I worked night shifts at the hospital as I studied for a textile degree. After the exam, I worked in a store during the day and studied marketing and economics at night.

A headhunter offered me a sales position within a financial institution. Knowing nothing about the industry, it sounded interesting and I accepted. My job was to build up a sales organization from scratch. It was tough, offered a lot of freedom and I loved it.

My husband and I moved abroad with our children and I engaged in the international school our children attended and I built up a Swedish department within the school curriculum.

We moved to a new country and I started a textile business, imported and sold fabrics and offered classes where I taught women to make beautiful lingerie. I was working from a pure pleasure of creation but knew I had more potential to fulfill.

As a textile raw material trader, my next job was to build up a trading organization from scratch within a worldwide company. Again, I jumped on something I knew nothing about, but it sounded intriguing and fun. The work included extensive travels to underdeveloped countries and it was challenging. I learned a lot and loved it.

My work/life situation was not sustainable. I loved my work but ignored my intuition and didn't want to face reality: I worked myself sick. I had worked so hard to build my career and it was difficult to give up my successful businesswoman persona.

Within a year, my life was turned upside down. I lost my career, moved back to Sweden and went through a rough divorce where I also lost most of my fortune. Long overdue, it was time for my soul-searching journey to delve deeper into philosophy, neuroscience and human behavior.

I spent hundreds of thousands of dollars on coaching, training and certifications. I developed my proprietary technique to quickly and profoundly create quantum shifts in a person's awareness and free them from negative emotions, limiting beliefs and old trauma.

Along with believing everything is possible, here's my recipe for Bliss:

1. Realize your strengths and fulfill your potential.

2. Trust your intuition and go for joy.

3. Dare to be curious, courageous and creative.

In hindsight, my break down was a blessing. For over 20 years, I've been supporting women to take full responsibility for their life and equip them with the right tools to excel in life and business in half the time and without Burnout.

I help them become the version of themselves that can say yes to their Boundless Brilliance, surpass every milestone and live the abundant life that they didn't even think was possible or dreamt of creating. That's my Bliss.

Lovely LaGuerre

Founder

Pure Heavenly Hair Boutique

Commercial - Luxury Real Estate Agent

https://lovelysellsvegas.com

https://pureheavenlyhair.com

https://www.linkedin.com/company/pure-heavenly-hair

https://www.instagram.com/pureheavenlyhair

https://www.facebook.com/Pure-Heavenly-Hair-Boutique-107278091130735

Lovely LaGuerre

Lovely LaGuerre is an entrepreneur, #1 international best-selling author of The Successful Woman's Mindset 21 Journeys to Success, a licensed commercial and luxury real estate agent. She is on a mission to help you turn your real estate investment dreams into a reality. She is also the Founder of Pure Heavenly Hair Boutique, a luxury beauty brand transforming, inspiring and empowering women to unleash their beauty inside and out. She is a member of NAIOP, CALV, NAR, GLVAR Association, Wealthy Women Inner Circle and many more! She resides in Las Vegas with her loving family.

Chapter 8

Beauty Is Powerful and Diverse

By Lovely LaGuerre

"My passion for the most sought industry"

No matter which international boundary you cross, regardless of the region you are born in and despite your distinct origins, you are beautiful. As a woman who is a fan of beauty and strength, I hope to encourage you all to discover your true beauty within. The reality of embracing beauty dawned upon me when I was noticeably young. When I had started dreaming about becoming someone in the beauty industry, I had said it out loud: "Be just the way you are." It worked for me. The first step towards reaching accomplishments is acceptance. Acceptance of yourself as the most beautiful person out there who deserves every good that exists in the world. I am talented and able enough to make things work my way, just the way I am.

As a teenager I vividly recalled going to the hair salon and looking at myself in the mirror and having the excitement of changing my hairstyle for special occasions. That experience of the salon has created a fiery passion and determination of becoming someone who contributes to being a part of the beauty industry.

I am proud to say my reach for greatness and my fate took a considerable leap forward ever since I started vocally reminding myself about it every day. With due time Pure Heavenly Hair Boutique was created. It is literally heaven on earth hair and beauty products for everyone who wants that luxury touch.

Becoming an entrepreneur is undoubtedly not a bed of roses. You must be passionate because without it, a body is just lingering around looking to be fed. Make your passion be your soul-food. Despite the troubling ups and down you will face, your firm belief will always make you rise-up floating like a winner. You will never drown if you swiftly switch to the pathway of being independent and self-reliant. As a businesswoman, you need to stand tall and ooze of confidence. You are a boss lady and the ones telling you that you are wrong, do not deserve a front seat in your life.

Through my journey there were some glitches to where I am today. I continuously was determined and craved success. More importantly my purpose has always been to share and to convey my knowledge.

I hope to encourage and inspire you all that everyone has the right to look beautiful in their own way. HAIR is one of the most sought-after beauty assets we have and want. Hair is a woman's true weapon. That propels me to create and be a part of the growing trend to contribute to the community of the beauty industry. Let no obstacles defeat you nor deter you from your growing transformation. You will reap the benefits if you keep aiming for that goal and not limit yourself. Reach further and leap higher.

Precisely, I hope to inspire the younger females to take away this lesson to know the beauty perception is to know your worth and self-confidence to not compare yourself to anyone. Just realize no one is YOU and only YOU hold the key to that power. Stay gorgeous and always be kind!

Cynde Canepa

Owner

A-Z Business Services

https://www.a-zbusinessservices.com

https://www.linkedin.com/in/tlcynde

https://www.instagram.com/cyndecanepa

https://www.facebook.com/cynde.canepa

Cynde Canepa, BS, EA, LTC#71491c, Founder & Financial Safety Coach for A-Z Business Services, est 1997. A-Z Business Services provides in-depth Administrative and Financial Assistance to guide your business to financial safety. Cynde is a Certified Oola Life & Money Coach, Certified Master Trainer, an Advanced Certified QuickBooks Pro Advisor, and is Enrolled to Practice Before The IRS. She has worked as a CPA Exam Candidate under a CPA performing all phases of public accounting, including audits, as well as holding responsibility as Controller and Vice President in the corporate world.

In 2017 Cynde met the Oola Guys at a Young Living Convention, the same time she received the call from her Doctor informing her she has a high grade pleomorphic Leiomyosarcoma cancer located on her dominate arm.

She maintains membership with the Daughters of the American Revolution (past Secretary & Treasurer), National Wildlife Federation, and the National Association of Family Childcare.

Chapter 9

Tips to a Successful Lifestyle

By Cynde Canepa

20 years ago, I was at the top of my game. After graduating with my business degree, I founded, A-Z Business Services, it was my passion. I was able to work from home and have a store front.

For most of my career I worked massive hours, helping others learn how to automate their business to do more of what they loved.

While I ironically, did not. Life was all about work. I desperately wanted more time with my family, but I was terrified of what would happen if I cut back my work hours.

Until a tumor finally forced me to.

I was not able to work because my tumor kept destroying my dominant arm. Also, the effects of radiation and the many different combinations of chemo had horrible effects on my body. I became forced into new lifestyle habits.

How could working LESS help me accomplish MORE?

I discovered 3 lifestyle habits that successful business owners do:

Tip #1: Get Enough Sleep.

It can be tempting to think of sleep like you do a checking account. If I just debit some sleep today, it's okay because I'll just make a sleep deposit this weekend.

It doesn't work that way. You can never make up the amount of sleep that you lose. That's because when you sleep, your brain cells are working to help de-stress you and to renew your mental energy.

If you want to succeed, you have to bring your A game. The number of hours that you sleep isn't the only thing that counts. The type of sleep that you get matters too. If you're in bed for seven or more hours but you're sleeping in fits, waking up and tossing and turning, then this affects your sleep cycle.

I used to wake early to start my day, worked all day until my body collapsed at night. I took my phone to bed with me because I felt I needed to be available if there was ever an emergency with my son. My sleep was interrupted. Either from clients texting me or with me waking up through the night thinking I have to get back to work before clients line up at my door wanting their bookkeeping or taxes.

Whenever your sleep cycle is interrupted, the quality of your sleep is not as restful. That means you aren't getting the physical or mental health benefits you should get from sleep.

Getting enough sleep can also help protect you from certain health risks.

Tip #2: Stress Relief

For example, you have to exercise. Working out isn't just about tightening up loose areas of the body or losing weight.

Exercise causes the release of dopamine and you feel better all over.

Tip #3: Quit what does not give you joy.

Everyone knows that in order to succeed, you can't quit. If what you're doing does not give you joy, quit doing it! Do what you love!

Patti Allred

CEO ~ #COINS Founder "Clear Online Income Now System!"

Allred Associates

http://pattiallred.com

https://www.linkedin.com/in/pattiallred

https://www.instagram.com/pattiallred

https://www.facebook.com/patti.allred

Patti Allred

Patti Allred is a self-made businesswoman, an online business solution specialist helping busy women and a few brave men unlock their success with a kick @$$ online business.

Born and raised in North Carolina Patti has been married to Bryon for over 35 years and has been extremely blessed to be a "Stay Home" Mom for over 32 years.

Patti is a strong believer in understanding that one does not have to have a "Formal Education" to make something of their lives and achieve their life goals. She believes that "Life Education" is more helpful in helping you reach your true dreams and be strong enough to see them through.

She and her husband allowed their children to choose the path that made them happy and didn't force them to go to college just because they were "supposed to" instead they helped them find what they enjoyed doing and guided them to follow their dreams. Their method has proven well with all three of their children as they couldn't be happier about their decisions and they all 3 are very successful in their chosen fields.

Chapter 10

WHY NOT ME?

By Patti Allred

Have you ever caught yourself saying "What About Me"? Probably more than once, right?

Let's think about what "What About Me" Really Means? Is it our cop out on life or is it our challenge to make changes?

We are all given our lives to live even if we are not living the life we thought we would be living. Truth is... It is still OUR LIFE.

What are we REALLY saying when we say "What About Me"?

*Why is MY LIFE so F'd up?

*Why are things going great for her and not me?

*Why is she always happy and I am always hurting?

*Why did my marriage fall apart and hers is great?

*Why did my kids turn out so different from hers?

*Why is that business working for her and I always fail?

Are any of those questions hitting home with you?

Have you ever found yourself totally caught up in the "What About Me" lifestyle mode?

It's ok to visit that place for a minute but staying there is totally NOT OK.

It's true, we never envisioned a life of being alone, no income, no support, being overweight, not healthy, no savings and always fighting with that damn voice in our heads telling us that things should be different but we somehow always choose the wrong path.

Yep, so many of us find ourselves in that rut and we just keep saying "WHAT ABOUT ME"???

Well newsflash, we all have 2 decisions.

#1 Keep asking "What About Me"? Or

#2 Get your ass in gear, find the positive things that you do have and allow them to help you go after that life that you desire.

Hard to hear? Yep! Simple to say but hard to do! I promise you that it's a hell of a lot easier than living in the "What About Me"? Lifestyle for the rest of your life. Can I get a witness??

So how can you make these changes? Start by getting 2 notebooks and some pretty pens (Pretty pens are not required but they make me happy and happy is always good!)

In one notebook list the things that you thought you would be doing at this point in your life in a color that makes you happy. In the other book, make a list of things that are making you ask "What About Me"?

Make sure you are completely honest so you can see, in black and white (or purple and pink!) what you are missing in your life.

Start weeding out those things that are bringing you down and add in things to help you get that life that will make you feel accomplished and put a smile on your face. Start there and don't stop.

You are the ONLY ONE who can make the changes that will help you truly be happy. You will never be happy until you make the necessary changes.

You got this. Forget the "Ready, Set, Go" and Just freakin GO.

You Are Worth It!

Change your "What About Me" to WHY NOT ME? and Enjoy Life!

It's way more fun!

Arlene Rivera

Public Figure, Speaker, Intuitive Coach, Medium and Energy Healer

The Arlene Inspires Organization

www.arleneinspires.com

www.arleneinspires.org

https://www.linkedin.com/in/nvarlenerivera

https://www.instagram.com/arleneinspires

https://www.facebook.com/arlene.rivera.399

Arlene is dedicated to putting the Spotlight on Healing. She is a fearless mental health, emotional and physical wellness advocate who passionately believes that healing is everyone's birthright. Arlene considers herself to be the "Erin Brockovich" of the mental health, mystical, holistic and overall wellness industries using her past legislative experience to join causes and influence to change laws. Uplifting and Serving Humanity, One Person and one cause at a time.

As a Public figure, Arlene is an influencer to be reckoned with. As a former TV personality and government community leader, she understands what it really takes to share the message of spiritual enlightenment, mental health, emotional and physical wellness with the masses. She does this through speaking engagements, consulting, intuitive coaching, advocacy, and volunteerism. She is very passionate about serving victims of sexual assault, domestic violence and human trafficking. Be sure to get a copy of Arlene's book "Raised by Intuition". It will change your life.

Chapter 11

Light Up with Purpose

By Arlene Rivera

How did I figure out what I want?

Well, I spent decades ignoring my inner wants and gifts. I wore a mask and wore it well. Society told me: I was perfect, successful, an overachiever, a great mom and I was even described as "a good egg"!

I loved to hear those things, I even began to believe it. However, the price I paid for all of that was too high.

I told myself little lies to justify my behaviors to keep up with society's expectations of me. I developed an unhealthy competitive mindset, I suffered from insomnia, my mind never stopped, I cared too much for what others thought of me and I questioned if I did too little or too much for others. Endless!

One day on my quest to find something outside of me, I had a breakthrough of self-actualization:

I realized I did not belong to myself. What I was looking for was not in a career, a partner, or a thing. It was inside of me. I was inspired to do more inner digging:

- I had to answer who is Arlene? The essence of her. Not how society viewed her.

- I had to write my own Eulogy. It helped me discern my life up to that point (a mind-blowing experience).

I also did a judgment detox to let go of judgments, the justified and unjustified ones. Including my self-talk! self-awareness and self-forgiveness are critical. #OwnershipAndKindness

Feeling light, like a feather - free of judgment!

I was now ready to brainstorm my passions without selling my soul for money or emotional obligation.

- I listed all those things that I would gladly do all day every day even without getting paid.

- I reflected on my "why" why do I want to do it?

- I asked myself, am I giving the truth about me to myself and others?

- How much time am I spending on my passions?

- What can I do right now to get closer to the next step?

- Do I want to do what it takes, or do I just want it?

Working hard at something does not mean it is worth more. If it doesn't flow let it go!

So I got disciplined! I rewired my behaviors and mindset:

- I now know that my behavior precedes my success.

- I remind myself I am my own CEO, average behavior will produce average results.

- I am disciplined with my time, from morning to evening.

- I created a routine with consistent and healthy habits.

- I invest in myself, for education and business.

- I am self accountable so I can be in business for myself.

- I am gentle with myself, have faith and I am impeccable with my words.

- **I BELIEVE IN MYSELF.** In life, we don't get what we ask for. **We get what we believe in**.

You can find more about my journey in my book *Raised By Intuition* releasing in 2022. **Don't forget to shine so brightly it blinds others!** :)

Ruth Furman

Principal

ImageWords Communications

https://www.ruthfurman.com

https://www.linkedin.com/in/ruthfurman

https://www.instagram.com/ruthiefurman

https://www.facebook.com/ImageWords-90861166609

Ruth Furman is a communications consultant and master connector. Her greatest joy is helping companies shine brighter by amplifying their stories and connecting them to opportunities.

If you're looking for the traditional PR agency, you'll want to keep searching. But if you want a one-of-a-kind marketing maven—full of creativity and quirks—who can introduce you to the right people at the right time, Ruth may be an ideal fit.

Through her three decades of experience, she watched clients become friends and friends become clients. She learned that results and relationships fuel her, and challenges quench her. Ruth has become a go-to resource for journalists seeking experts. She is energized by being the biggest cheerleader and strongest advocate for her clients, past and present.

Based in Las Vegas, Ruth has the curiosity of a journalist, the enthusiasm of a publicist and the strategic mind of a marketing consultant.

Chapter 12

Find Your Joy with Kindness, to Yourself and Others

By Ruth Furman

As a public relations agency owner, connections are my business. I link sources with news reporters, ideas with outlets. In 20 years of doing this work (I recently celebrated my business anniversary with cake!), I've realized these connections help me as much as they help other people, especially when last-minute requests jumble my routine.

Take the other day, when I just could not find my keys. I looked everywhere. On tables, under magazines and in jackets. I even dumped my purse. Nothing. When my friend came to my house, bearing cups of coffee and fresh eyes, we found the keys. In minutes.

When I misplace things, it's a sign I need to slow down. Over the years, I've been guilty of moving way too fast. Pausing makes perfect every time.

If I'm rushed to complete a project, it's often because of a bad yes. I've made many of those since launching my company in 2001. I've learned from everyone, even finding joy in most of them.

I've learned to take the wisdom and move on, life's too short to obsess over errors you've made or will make. As a greeting card I saw recently reminded me, "Don't be fearful of what could go wrong. Get excited about what may go right."

I embrace my newfound ability to look ahead and not behind. This has come with cutting myself some slack. As Oprah Winfrey said, "Forgiveness is giving up the hope that the past could be any different. It is accepting the past for what it was and using this moment and this time to help yourself move forward."

Absolutes I've learned over the years:

Avoid the "b" word: Saying you're busy isn't a badge of honor. It just makes the other party feel bad.

Respond quickly. If you tell people you'll call back or send something, do it. Call them before they have to call you to follow up. If you're running behind, reach out before the deadline, not after.

Talk: Be willing to have a conversation. Texts and emails are a breeding ground for hurt feelings and misunderstandings.

As important as it is to connect with other people, it's important to connect with yourself. This means leaving yourself time to reflect, free of pinging phones or scrolling social media feeds. It also means leaving work at work. Years ago, in my first job out of college, a co-worker told me he got his hair cut on company time because it grew on company time. Also, outsource as many tasks as you can, as often as you can, so you have room to do what you do best.

Be kind to yourself by focusing on what you can do. Comparing yourself to others will kill your joy every time.

Above all, laugh at yourself.

My friend and I laughed when those keys turned up. We toasted the moment with our coffees. Every little victory matters.

Sherri Leopold

Owner

Dream Big with Sherri Leopold

https://sherrileopold.com

https://thrivewithsherri.com

https://linkedin.com/sherrileopold

https://instagram.com/sherrileopold

https://facebook.com/dreambigwithsherrileopold

Sherri Leopold is a Mentor, 2 time International Bestselling Author, Speaker, Founder and CEO of Dream Big with Sherri Leopold. She is a television host of the show Outside the Box with Sherri Leopold on ISheTV and has worked in the Network Marketing/Direct Selling industry for 23 years, sharing her expertise in speaking, mentoring, and team building.

Sherri released her first book in June of 2019 called Self-Bullying: What To Do When the Bully is YOU! As Leader of the Stop Self-Bullying Movement, Sherri released her program called WOW Warriors. This Stop Self- Bullying training eradicates negative self-talk and teaches people to Stand UP and Stand OUT!

Sherri hosts the television show called Outside the Box with Sherri Leopold on ISheTV where she shines a light on servant leaders making a difference in the world. You can contact her at SherriLeopold2@gmail.com.

Chapter 13

Dream BIG, Believe BIGGER!

By Sherri Leopold

As a network marketer for 20+ years, I have met amazing women. I have also met many women who have stopped dreaming about the life they deserve. They gave up and settled. I aim to change that. I want to be a catalyst for women to begin to dream again. Where does someone start when they want to do this?

After months of soul searching in 2018, recovering from a life altering, soul crushing experience where my character was attacked, I had to learn to dream again myself. I began to realize there was a pattern emerging with strong powerful women I followed. I desired to be that strong powerful woman again. The women who lived successful, fulfilled lives were the ones who loved themselves most. I don't mean an arrogant, boastful sort of self-centered view of themselves, but a confident, self-worthy, powerful internal compass that guided them. These women stand UP and stand OUT! My mission is to empower ALL women to do just that. I want to help women stand UP and stand OUT as the unrepeatable miracle they were born as! This is a process that can be learned because I did just that! We don't fall out of the womb confident and self-assured. We don't fall out as mothers, wives, or executives either. This is something that can be learned and mastered. We must first CHOOSE to dream BIG and accept that we matter.

Dreaming BIG is about enlarging your vision of what is possible. Vision cast is an exercise I use with my clients. Imagine yourself 5-10 years down the road at the pinnacle of success. What does it look like? What house are you living in? What cars are you driving?

What is the lifestyle you have created? Once you know the answers to these questions, you can then move to the skill set you need to have to create this desired life. When you identify what you truly desire in life, knowing who you are is the essential next step to get what you want.

What are the strengths you have, the talents that bring you great joy when using them? This IS what makes you uniquely you. This is one of the biggest steps in the process to learning to dream BIG! When you understand that your exclusive DNA is like no one else on the planet, you understand the magnitude of how special you really are. There is no one that has your unique way of speaking, thinking; no one who has your belief systems and experiences. There is only one beautiful YOU! We could both be speakers on personal development focused on mindset, and we would sound nothing alike. We each have our own experiences, educational backgrounds, and relationships that impact our words. We might resonate with someone, but we will never be just alike.

I invite you to Dream Big, Believe BIGGER, and to know YOU are an unrepeatable Miracle exactly as you are today!

Pamela Kurt

Coach

Best Version Of You LLC

www.bestversionyou.com

www.yourcoachpam.com

https://www.linkedin.com/in/pamela-kurt-41a26ba

https://www.instagram.com/best_version_you

https://www.facebook.com/Best-Version-You-103772311530954

Pamela D. Kurt is a Life Coach for professional women and an attorney. She lives on the Shores of Lake Erie, Ohio with her fiancé and their dogs Bailey and Bella. She has an adult son that who is an award-winning movie director and producer. She currently owns her own law firm. As a business owner, she is also very active in her community and has held several leadership roles. She has been a guest speaker on various forums and an author of a best seller, The Successful Women's Mindset, 21 Journeys to Success.

Her passion is to support and to empower women to be the best they can! The most personal enjoyment is when her clients find their own way. Her private practice to empower women to be their best. BE THE BEST YOU! Her coaching program has allowed her clients on a powerful self-discovery journey. She is currently accepting new private coaching clients. Please contact her at BestVersionYou.com for a consultation to see if this program is right for you.

Chapter 14

Take a moment

By Pamela Kurt

I started my life journey in a small rural community. I didn't come from a wealthy family, but I wanted more. There was always a burning desire inside of me for a greater purpose. I got married young and had a beautiful son and got divorced young. Then I started this self-awareness journey. I went back to school and obtained my Associates, Bachelors, Master's and Doctorate while being a single struggling Mother. I wanted more and I wanted to show my son you can be and do anything.

It was easy for me to "show my son". That gave me the momentum to continue to strive and to get through everyday challenges. I think a lot of times as successful women, we can easily take on more and put our children first or anyone else first. There is always chaos and there is always something to do. Ask yourself this: Can't you always find time if someone else needs you? The answer is almost always. YES! But we need to take a moment.

What I found for me is that in the chaos and daily tasks, I need to consciously take selfcare steps daily. It's so easy to build in a daily routine for most tasks. From getting kids on the bus. to packing lunches and to following up on emails. When the focus is on you, it's a little harder. Daily I take a break, I need those moments. Taking those moments are worth it and you deserve it.

Daily, do you pray? Mediate? Journal? We know those are great self-care things and most of us have great intentions to do those tasks daily and even commit to them. We are going to be balanced and take care of ourselves. We are going to start to say "no" more often and do better with self-care and planning and eating and exercise and yet literally taking time for yourself is hard! Some people even beat themselves up about not being able to carve out daily time for self-care. Self-care then becomes another "task" and item on the "to do list". Unfortunately, most often if time is scarce, this is the one "to do" item that stays on the list undone.

Let's try to start small… take a moment. STOP! Close your eyes. Do it right now. Breathe. Try to think of nothing. Of course, that is easier said than done but STOP! and if you need to simply count. Count at least to 50. You have taken a moment and those moments help to regroup and have a moment of peace. In my businesses, I find women that are usually exhausted and burned out. And simply searching for fulfillment and peace. I started a coaching business to help professional women become the best version of themselves. Find those moments and feel peace. It doesn't mean you have to quit your job or change careers. It simply means to elevate you to be the best version of you.

Ginger Allen

CEO

Your Marketing Liaison

https://yourmarketingliaison.com

https://www.linkedin.com/in/yourmarketingliaison

https://www.instagram.com/yourmarketingliaison

https://www.facebook.com/YourMarketingLiaison

As the owner, chief business development consultant and strategic planner for Your Marketing Liaison, Ginger Allen oversees a marketing team of like-minded entrepreneurs to bring first-class representation to each of her clients. We are a full-fledged marketing agency offering everything from websites and social media management, branding and strategy, logos and brochures, field marketing and networking, online advertising, and traditional advertising mediums.

Ginger is the Past Co-President of the Clark County Medical Society Alliance and is affiliated with many Non-Profits and Community Organizations. Ginger is also passionate about supporting women owned businesses and started a Facebook Group called the Network of Women Business Owners.

Chapter 15

Passion & Purpose vs Money & Success

By Ginger Allen

As a serial entrepreneur and a recovering alcoholic, I started my first business at 21 years old, a mobile espresso bar. I then built a bio-medical supply company, a real estate, title and mortgage company. Today I own a marketing agency in Las Vegas, NV.

When I began my journey as an entrepreneur, I thought that making money was the key to my happiness. I aspired to make six figures by the time I was 30. When I reached that goal at 33 years old, I found that something still seemed to be missing: happiness. I was successful on the outside, but my drinking increased heavily every day. Entrepreneurship is stressful and I used it as an excuse for my inability to cope. When other people saw me, they thought I was living the good life. I had a successful business, a home on the ocean and drove a new Mercedes. I was also living in denial.

Until one day, my Mom, who is my best friend, looked at me and said, "I think you might be an alcoholic." My immediate reaction: "Who? Me? Have you seen my success?" I was not ready to face my reality. Then 2008 hit, the real estate market crashed and I lost everything. I got divorced and I got sober. That year, I learned what it meant to actually do what you love.

Learning to do what I love meant learning balance, sobriety, focusing on my physical and mental health, my family, real friends, peace and serenity. Yes, making money and being successful is important, but not at the expense of the most important things in life. So, I shifted my perspective and I put those things first.

In 2014, after getting healthy and happy, I looked at all my years of experience and realized it was the marketing and advertising of each business that I loved so much. Your Marketing Liaison was born. My passion became about helping others achieve success and grow their businesses. I do believe that if you love what you do, it won't feel like work but you also have to be personally happy for it all to work.

Today, I love what I do. I also loved all the businesses I owned and operated before, but the difference was that I didn't love myself. My self-worth was based on monetary success only and I know now that there is so much more to life than money. Today, I work hard to have a work-life balance. I put my sobriety first. I do Pilates, volunteer for non-profits, make time for family, travel and I am saving for retirement. Making the most money is no longer the main priority for me. I now focus on being happy first and letting the rest work itself out. I am grateful to say that I have found my personal purpose and passion in life!

Andrea Clark

CEO

Medical Revenue, MD

https://www.medicalrevenuemd.com

https://www.linkedin.com/in/andreaclarkmrmd

https://www.instagram.com/medicalrevenuemd

https://www.facebook.com/MedicalRevenueMD

Andrea started her career in the banking industry and quickly excelled over her counterparts all over the nation, making her one of the most trusted bankers in the medical industry. Her training and experience results in a master's degree in finance and she has learned proven strategies for coaching and managing teams. She understands the dynamics of a medical practice and has had amazing success increasing profits by assessing their medical billing, systematizing their operations, and overseeing their finances.

She has a record of uncovering thousands of dollars and is known as the "Financial Powerhouse" in the medical community. In 2015 she started Medical Revenue, MD – a full revenue cycle management company with services that include practice management, medical billing, credentialing, and staffing. Since then, she has been awarded for 100 Top Women of Las Vegas three years in a row, Top 40 Under 40, and Top 20 Entrepreneurs of 2020.

Chapter 16

From the Softball Field to the Medical Field

By Andrea Clark

Growing up as an athlete, I thought that I was invincible. I dedicated my life to the game, working out 2 times a day and 6 days a week. My hard work and efforts paid off as I received several college recruitment offers and the opportunity to try out for the 2000 Women's Olympic Team. Then, my dedication to the sport came to an abrupt halt and my softball career was over. During a tournament I suffered an injury and was told I would never play again. I was in and out of doctors' offices and had to undergo surgery and two years of physical therapy. As I spent endless hours in waiting rooms and had multiple doctor visits, I was able to observe so much of what was going on around me. This is where my passion for the medical field came from and my first epiphany into my future.

After my injury I continued to college. With no scholarships, I began working in banking and quickly became one of the top 5 business bankers on the west coast. As I worked my way up the ranks, I utilized my work ethic and perseverance that I learned from sports to put me high within a man's world of finance. At the peak of my banking career, I was faced with another obstacle. I was in a car accident that led to a massive back surgery. My spirits were crushed and I had to be sidelined while I healed from the back surgery. Again,

I sat in doctors waiting rooms. After six years of rehabilitation, multiple doctor visits with different specialists and hours of my life I would never get back, I personally witnessed horrendous wait times, physician burn out and staff who were over worked and underpaid. I saw that this resulted in poor patient care, negative patient experience and angry staff. I decided something in the medical industry had to change. This is when my business and my passion were born.

As I built Medical Revenue, MD I faced many obstacles. As a woman I was shut down more than I was given opportunities. I faced the hurdle of working with individuals who have an extensive education and I had to tell them everything they learned about running a practice was wrong. No matter how many times I was shut out or knocked down, I would reflect on the characteristics of my athletic career, get up and continue forward. I knew the knowledge I had was industry changing and over the years it has proven so. I've learned that those who become successful move against the grain, think outside the box and never give up. I have this mentality within my company and with all the doctors and medical practices I work with. Because of my perseverance with all the obstacles I have faced in life. I never gave up on my passion. That passion now allows doctors to focus on the patient care, have more time for their personal life and be confident they have the best staff who are providing excellent patient experience.

Brianna Dotson

CEO

The Coaching Company LLC

https://www.linkedin.com/in/briannafdotson

https://www.instagram.com/briannafdotson

https://www.facebook.com/briannafdotson

As a high achiever, people pleaser and perfectionist, Brianna knows what it feels like to allow self-doubt to crowd valuable headspace. Brianna was regularly holding herself back at work and allowing that pesky negative self-dialogue to take over. Because of this, she rarely shared her voice in meetings.

Brianna's greatest glow-up was stepping into her corporate power and finding her voice in the workplace. Once she overcame self-doubt and realized her full potential, Brianna began assisting other women to do the same. Now you will find Brianna empowering high achievers to ditch self-doubt, feel empowered at work and enjoy life.

She believes women deserve to get paid lots of money to do what they love. Brianna helps others achieve this by guiding them to discover their own passion and purpose.

Her motto being: You should never have to give up happiness for a paycheck.

Chapter 17

Ditch Societal Norms & Do What You Love

By: Brianna F. Dotson

Society tells us to graduate high school, go to college, debt is okay, get a high paying job. Do all of this so you can afford the fancy clothes, fancy apartment and the fancy car but what most people tend to leave out is that you may not be happy. It's okay because everyone hates their job, right?

I followed that same path. Before graduating college, I already achieved a certain level of what society deems as 'successful'. I was chosen for a highly sought-after internship abroad and spent a semester working in Lima, Peru. Right after my return to the states, I was selected for another internship where I found myself leading meetings and globetrotting with an automotive supplier.

Before the age of 25, I realized I could really achieve whatever I desired in the corporate setting. I found myself in a position that I really enjoyed but I felt something was missing.

Next thing I know, I was signed up for a coaching certification course. To this day, I have no idea how I really got there or what led me to that idea. Within 8 intensive weeks, I became a Certified Professional Coach.

I will just do this on the side because it is something I enjoy.

I will not charge too much, I have a decent paying job.

Those are the things I told myself when first starting out but silly me, I did not realize that people make good money by coaching and doing what they love. Coaching was so new to me and I had no idea what was possible.

Me being an entrepreneur? No way.

I do not know anyone who has done that before.

Who am I to coach people?

People will judge me.

I literally gave myself all the reasons why I wouldn't be successful rather than all the reasons why I could be. As soon as I started believing in myself, I started expanding my coaching practice more than I thought possible. Now I help women just like you find clarity in their career paths and feel empowered in the workplace.

If there is one thing that I learned from all of this, it is that whether you tell yourself you can or you can't, you are right. If you tell yourself that you cannot do it, you will find all the reasons to validate that idea. The opposite is true as well. Once you begin to tell yourself that you can, you will find all the validation in the world that you can be successful.

Even if you have all the success in your corporate career and you are not happy, you do not have to stay there. Find what makes you happy, find your version of success. Success looks and feels different on all of us, and success is not a one size fits all.

Are you living out your own personal success story?

Sasha Nizgoda

Licensed Real Estate Salesperson

Sasha Nizgoda – Triplemint

https://sashasellsnj.com

https://www.linkedin.com/in/sashanizgoda

https://www.instagram.com/sashasellsnj

https://www.facebook.com/SashaSellsNJ

Sasha Nizgoda is an experienced real estate agent with a decade of experience. She is committed to her clients, recognizing the trust her clients place in her and works hard to exceed their expectations.

She began her real estate career in Las Vegas, where she oversaw each transaction that her firm conducted. Sasha's roles spanned creative marketing, strategic direction, lead generation, recruiting, managing agents, and working closely with buyers, sellers, and investors. Sasha is an expert in the buying, selling, and leasing process and has drove her company to great recognition and success in the Las Vegas area.

In her spare time, Sasha can be found volunteering. She has been on the board of directors and chair of the Glass Class for the Anti-Defamation League. Sasha also volunteers in the autism community, having been a member of FEAT of Southern Nevada. She has expanded her volunteer work to the women's community in hopes to try to help women in need.

Sasha lives in Hoboken with her husband, her three young daughters, and their Chiweenie, Diva. Her generous spirit, warm sense of humor, and dynamic energy are a huge contribution to her success as a Realtor and to her pursuit to uplift and support women.

Chapter 18

Dare To Dream

By Sasha Nizgoda

Growing up, I was raised by a single mother who worked tirelessly just to make ends meet. Most of my childhood memories were from spending time with her at work. I would sit by her computer, play with office supplies and fantasize about life as a woman in the workforce. Although I wish I had more memories with her sitting on the beach or traveling around the world carefree, I am thankful to have truly witnessed what it means to be a working mom. She was constantly reinventing herself in her rotating roles as a wage earner, parent and a woman.

We are told from a young age that we can be whatever we want as adults, but that is only theoretically true. The reality is that we often feel hemmed in by what society expects of us. My mother always encouraged me to think and speak freely. She knew she couldn't hold me back when I felt strongly about a topic but would guide me to do so in an appropriate yet powerful way.

I watched her reinvent herself many times, but it seemed like an impossible task when it was time for me to become a woman myself without my mother's guidance. Unfortunately, she passed away when I was 21 years old. It's not always easy to work full time, raise a family and carve time for yourself, but I have found my balance and

I hope my words can help other women trying to find theirs. I will share a few tips that have helped me become successful in my career. I share them in the hope my mother's lessons can continue to inspire.

First of all: let go of the guilt! We are working mothers, we are women who are caretakers for our parents or family members, we are women dealing with depression and trying to make it through the day. There is only so much one person can do, so be kind to yourself and let the guilt go for things that are out of your control. Be forgiving of yourself like you would be for someone else.

Set realistic goals! I cannot stress this enough. Come up with a clear plan to achieve those goals and take action persistently. There are many tools to keep you organized, so find what works for you. Hold yourself accountable and take action.

Like my mom, reinvent yourself as many times as you need. Don't be afraid to change yourself over and over again. There is no true timeline for following your passions in life. So, if you are not happy with where you live move. If you are fifty years old and have always dreamed of having a degree, go back to school and get that diploma. You never age out of humor or joy, so cultivate it when and where you can!

Finally, to all the girls, young adults and women all around the world: be your true, authentic self. Don't you dare dim your light in order to make someone else feel better. When life gets tough, remember that little girl inside of you with big dreams. Don't let her down because she deserves it and that means you do too.

Stacey Lockhart

Executive Director

HopeLink of Southern Nevada

https://www.linkedin.com/in/staceymarsh

https://www.facebook.com/stacey.lockhart64

Lockhart is a non-profit executive who's spent her 30+-year career serving in leadership roles within nonprofits and higher education institutions in Washington, Alaska, Colorado, and Nevada. Through her leadership and strong service to the community, Lockhart's personal mission is to help others. She has a long and successful track record in fundraising, raising millions of dollars for the organizations she's been a part of.

Today, Lockhart serves as the executive director with HopeLink of Southern Nevada, a nonprofit with locations in Henderson and Las Vegas, Nevada with a mission of preventing homelessness, preserving families, and providing hope.

Prior to joining HopeLink, Lockhart served as the executive director of The Shade Tree, a shelter for homeless, abused women, and children. In her first year there, Lockhart spearheaded a $2.5 million dollar renovation which entailed upgrading the 40,000 square foot facility and 5-acre campus located in downtown Las Vegas. She also helped the organization attain financial stability.

Chapter 19

Why are we all so different?

By Stacey Lockhart

Recently my sister said, "I was just thinking… our brother is all about taking care of his family, you're all about taking care of everyone else and I'm more about taking care of me. Why are we all so different?"

Why are we all so different?

I literally stumbled into my career path, it wasn't something I planned and it wasn't intentional at first and it wasn't even what I had spent 4 years getting a degree for! One day I realized that I had found something I was good at and loved doing. I was 26 at the time and when I came to this realization. I'd found my sense of place or you could say my passion caring for others by connecting people and their money to the causes and organizations they cared about. At my core, I am what is called a "Fundraiser or Development Professional."

Through fundraising over the past 30+ years, I have had the honor of helping people with disabilities live independent lives, provided access and opportunity to those who want a college education, attracted financial support for world class athlete training and development so they could have their shot at the Olympics, provided a safe haven for abused and homeless women and children and most recently, preventing homelessness of families who find themselves in crisis, many times, no fault of their own.

Once you find your own sense of place or passion, do everything you can to train and educate yourself and build a network of incredible mentors and peers who will help you succeed. Then nurture these relationships throughout your life.

Never stop learning! There are programs at colleges and universities and local chapters in the community that are part of national organizations specifically designed for people who want to work, or want to advance in nonprofit fundraising, nonprofit administration, supervision, case management, social work and so much more.

Network! It's how things get done! Attend professional events, Chamber of Commerce networking events. Build your tribe and build your reputation. I have always said that you don't raise the kind of money that transforms lives sitting behind a desk. GO! Get up and get out from behind the desk!

Be willing to put in the time and effort. Push past hard days and celebrate the wins. Be proud of each step you take towards reaching your goals.

What is success? How do you know when you've achieved it? How do you know you're meant to do it?

For me it was the day I realized that I had found something that I was good at and that I loved doing. Over the years, anytime I think about what else I would want to do if I decided it was time for a change, I always come back to the same answer, NOTHING! I LOVE what I do, I look forward to each day and at the end of the day I feel good about myself and the work I've done.

I've concluded that in answer to my sister's question, we're all so different because the world needs us to be. We all bring something special to the world and there is no wrong answer, only the one that's right for you.

Go forth and embrace your WHY!

Dr. Vicki Coleman

President/CEO

The Coleman Group & The Anger Doctor

http://www.AngerDr.com

http://www.TheColemanGroup.org

http://www.linkedin.com/in/doccole

http://www.instagram.com/AngerDoctor

http://www.facebook.com/DrVickiDColeman

Dr. Vicki D. Coleman is an Internationally Recognized Behavioral Health Specialist, Online Professor of Psychology, Amazon #1 Best Selling Author, and Educator.

A former Tenured Professor at Purdue University in West Lafayette, IN, Dr. Coleman has held positions in mental health, food and beverage, and transportation, including Northwestern University and American Airlines. She conducts research on anger management, career development, sports psychology, addictions, and multicultural and diverse populations, with several inter/national refereed publications.

As President/CEO of management consulting firms, The Anger Doctor & The Coleman Group, Dr. Coleman travels globally, providing consultation for educational institutions, business, industry, government, professional associations, and community organizations.

A native of Detroit, Michigan, Dr. Coleman earned a Bachelor's degree in Political Science and a Master's in U.S. and Latin American History from The University of Iowa; a Master's in Counselor Education from Northern Illinois University; and a Doctorate in Counseling Psychology from Rutgers University.

Chapter 20

"Be Your Own Superhero!"

By Dr. Vicki D. Coleman

Throughout my career, as I carefully examined role models, mentors and heroes/sheroes in my life, it finally dawned on me that I can "Be My Own Superhero!" Yes, you can and do not focus on others' success and accomplishments as the barometer. Do your own thing and set the standard! Superhero status is a new mindset and way to facilitate personal and professional growth.

So, how did I come to this epiphany, or realization? As an academician, researcher and Executive Coach, one strategy utilized that has helped others, is to analyze their Career Development. Why did it take me so long to apply this to my own circumstances? Well, as the saying goes, the doctor cannot heal herself!? Maybe???

Below is a summary of the Career Development Model (Coleman, 2008 Coleman & Barker, 1992), or paradigm that I utilize and recommend, when considering developing your own Superhero mindset. One important reminder is that this is a *process,* not to be completed in one session or engagement and it might require professional assistance to facilitate the *process.*

Introduction/Orientation

An introduction to the concept and process of career development and vocational psychology is the initial step. Career development is an ongoing, lifelong process which focuses on the acquisition of information and skills about self and the environment.

Self-Assessment

This step requires an in-depth assessment and evaluation of one's values, core beliefs, interests, abilities, strengths, personality, goals and world view, among others.

Decision Making

There are several models which highlight the decision-making process, including various strategies and styles. Some identify seven steps with determining the decision and gathering information, as I believe is the most critical, as these serve as the foundation for establishing alternatives. What is critical is that individuals can discern themes and patterns in their decision-making styles, asking the question, "Are the strategies and styles utilized yielding positive decisions?"

Educational, Occupational & Community Information

There is a wealth of information related to occupations and careers in the global economy and the educational requirements to pursue these opportunities. Most communities provide access to resources via colleges/universities, nonprofit organizations, libraries and municipal, county and state entities, to name a few. The federal government is also an excellent resource.

Preparation for Work, Leisure & Retirement

In the 21st century global economy, one can actually plan and prepare for the workplace, leisure time and retirement. Oftentimes, retirement means leaving one career and entering another, possible entrepreneurship.

There are a myriad of tools and resources available. Many are online to assist in helping an individual with the career development process.

To begin the career development process, one of my favorite tools is the Lifeline Exercise (Coleman, 1998) that is an opportunity to look at the past, present and future, focusing on themes, trends and patterns related to thinking, decision making and behavior.

If one adheres to the aforementioned Model and recommendations, being your own Superhero and developing a new mindset, may be in the immediate horizon!

References

Coleman, V.D. (2008). A model of career development: 21st Century applications.

Australian Career Practitioner, Spring, 19, 19-20.

Coleman, V.D. (1998). Lifeline. In Rosenthal, H.G. (Ed.), *Favorite counseling techniques.* Washington, D.C.: Taylor & Francis.

Coleman, V.D. & Barker, S.A. (1992). A model of career development for a multicultural workforce. *International Journal for the Advancement of Counseling, 15,* 187-195.

Renata Moise

Reiki Master & Teacher/ Coach

Healing Waters Spa and Wellness Center

www.myhealingwaterslv.com/reiki-energy-clearing

www.etsy.com/shop/ReikiAndJewelryShop

https://www.linkedin.com/in/renata-moise

https://www.instagram.com/renata_reikihealer_realestate

https://m.facebook.com/HealYourselfHealthAndWellnessCenter

Renata is an experienced and Certified Reiki Master & Teacher, and Chakra healer.

She has been certified and practiced Reiki since 2012. She has an extensive understanding and deep passion for healing through divine love and universal life force energy. She coaches, empowers and guides people and children through their healing and spiritual journey to improve any and all aspects of their life to become the best version of themselves.

She knew in her heart that it was her destiny to become a Reiki Master Teacher and share the gift of Reiki healing art and knowledge with others. She always welcomes and is open to anyone or any groups of people who wish to learn and experience Reiki through private sessions, group meditations, workshops and her Reiki practitioner certification classes of all 4 levels.

In the past, she has built a successful Real Estate Business and managed Trade Show associates Nationally and Internationally, focusing on helping companies and her clients to accomplish their goals for over 10 years. As a part of her Real estate professional recognition she was named as the #3 Sales Executive at her Berkshire Hathaway Nevada office in 2018 as well as nominated and awarded Top 100 Women in Real Estate for 2017 by MyVegas Magazine. Renata also likes to be involved and help the community and worked as an organizer for various charitable functions. Staying active she has been a sponsored athlete and competitive runner since 2010 winning many medals, trophies and awards, she is a three-time qualifier for the Boston Marathon.

Always wanting to stay busy and involved, she was awarded Camp Counselors USA certificate for summer season 2000 at Blue Star Camps when she first came to USA as Exchange Program Student – a United States Government designed Exchange Visitor Program witch brings young people from overseas to the US for a four-month program in American summer camps to gain educational and cultural experiences, and to promote the general interest of international exchange. She was born in Slovakia and is also fluent in Slovak and Czech languages.

Chapter 21

Face Your Fears and Do It Anyway

By Renata Moise

While studying at the City University I was one of the chosen students to come to America as an exchange student. I was excited and scared at the same time but deep down in my heart I felt a burning desire to Face those Fears and do it anyway. I asked myself "What's the worst thing that could happen? I could always return to where I was before?".

It was tough without family here and no money. I didn't speak, write or read English back then and self-learned on my own. Along my journey in America, I found myself lost and stuck. I was ready for a positive change, healing and overall transformation in many aspects of my life. I started creating and building my new dreams I had passion for, a real estate business and an international conventions and modeling business.

On a journey toward overcoming some past traumatic events, I also found Reiki. With each healing experience, my conviction grew stronger and Reiki became a part of my every day way of life. I found my healing abilities invaluable not only in my self-healing and transformation, but also in helping in the healing process of my beloved mother overseas and others who deal with pain and suffering.

As a part of my transformation, I also decided to start training for a marathon. Through my consistent trainings I have become a competitive athlete. I have passionately run and competed for many reasons, won many races, medals and awards. April 2018, I qualified for the Boston marathon for the 3rd time.

A month later I was attacked and body slammed to the ground by an attacker injuring my arm, lower back, hip and knee. My whole life changed in a wink of an eye. My running career was over.

I was diagnosed with post traumatic depression and anxieties and was prescribed medication. Since the attacker was a male, I had to face the fears every day since I worked in a male dominated industry. Reiki played a huge part of my healing process, recovery and rehabilitation. From my transformational experiences I knew more than ever that I wanted to share Reiki with others through my Reiki healing practice, private healing sessions and programs, group meditations, healing circles, workshops and Reiki practitioner certification trainings of all 4 levels.

I start my daily routine with Reiki spiritual protection, Reiki meditation and prayer, positive mindset exercises, listening to empowering music like the album "Epic" by Las Vegas Symphony Orchestra.

How do you empower yourself daily?

What if the challenges we are facing today are not happening to us but for us? To learn, to grow, even inspire others. What do you do next time your fears are looking you straight in your eyes? First thing you can do is "Recognize and Acknowledge" them. Be aware they are here to test you. Next, ask yourself "What is the worst thing that could happen when I face those Fears and do it anyway? What you see as scary at first might actually end up being a great opportunity for growth and inner strength. Third, "Face it, Replace it and Repeat it". By facing it and actually getting a good outcome, you will automatically replace it with Trust and Confidence. Keep repeating this process and you will find yourself unstoppable!

Adriana Luna Carlos

Co-Founder

She Rises Studios

http://www.adrianalunadesigns.com

https://sherisesstudios.com

https://www.linkedin.com/company/she-rises-studios

https://www.instagram.com/sherisesstudios

https://www.facebook.com/sherisesstudios

Adriana Luna Carlos is a bold and brave entrepreneur currently residing in Las Vegas, Nevada. She is a spirited and intelligent woman focusing on helping others alike to rise and become unafraid of successes. Adriana graduated with honors from Pasadena High School in 2012 and went on to attend UCLA College of Medicine to become a cardiologist. She realized her passion was in graphic & web arts and leading women like herself to turn their passion into a lifestyle and career.

She founded Adriana Luna Designs in 2013 and co-founded She Rises Studios in 2020, amidst a global pandemic. With a deep understanding of insecure idiosyncrasies, Adriana has found a way to break through these boundaries. Adriana now educates, celebrates, and mentors other women to ascend and emerge into fearless women leaders. She challenges us all to accept nothing less than a life of excellence!

Chapter 22

It's Time For A REAL Self-Talk

By Adriana Luna Carlos

I've always been a driven individual because I was raised in a family of entrepreneurs. My parents, aunts and grandparents all had a business or side hustle at some point in their lives. Growing up in this lifestyle gave me such a precious gift that I can never put a price tag on. At a young age my family taught me what perseverance was and how to earn what you desire in life. Not only did they teach me to create my own wealth but to help others do the same for themselves.

Everyone is meant for something great in this world, God gave you a life and a precious one at that.

Never waste your life, your talents, your smarts, your kindness, or your love. Do your best to fulfill your worth and abilities and you will be a happier person for it. The most important thing in life is not money but a fulfillment of purpose, YOUR purpose.

I love the saying that "success is when opportunity meets preparation". Now break that down and REALLY listen to what it means. They are simple words individually but an even more powerful life-changing phrase when placed together. What is something that you thought you would never achieve or could become and now you are that! It's not LUCK! It was preparation MEETING an opportunity.

Even if you don't know what you want to do today, that's okay! You have time so go get started. Write down all the things that make you happy, see what they can all branch out into and then research them.

Are you willing to sacrifice to get the desired outcome that you want? Cultivate your dreams and find your clarity by developing your gifts and talents.

Here's how you can start: Cultivate your dreams, establish clarity and develop your calling.

For me, I really love helping people and I have a business mind. Put that together and you get an Assistant Executive Director to a Non-Profit organization and Co-Founder of a Women Lead Global Network. These are amazing opportunities that did NOT come to me easily. I worked hard for these careers and I sacrificed a lot. I've spent months of time reading, researching, expanding my skills and brushing up on old ones and you know what? I am a happier person and I feel so blessed and grateful for the opportunities. Many people tell me I am lucky and I've decided that that is not true. I've earned my happiness and I want so badly to help others see their worth.

Today you MUST stand up and recognize your worth because I do. I see you for who you are, for what you can become and I believe in you. Practice having a strong heart and mind, set boundaries, learn from your mistakes and make new ones to get to that higher place. Although I may have achieved a lot out of my 27 years of life, I still have so much on my list to better myself and continuously find my passion.

HOW ABOUT YOU? Get started on your list. I'll be here if you need me!

Michelle Perkins

Executive Coach

MP Coaching

https://www.linkedin.com/in/michellerperkins

https://www.instagram.com/michellerperkins

https://www.facebook.com/michelle.perkins.980

Michelle Perkins specializes in Executive Leadership and Training. She is a coach, speaker, and successful leader with years of leadership experience in the corporate world. For over 15 years, she has provided support to women who are struggling with the complexities of life. Through her own personal experiences, she has gained an understanding and appreciation of the challenges that women face in an ever-changing world.

Her clients are extraordinary, high achieving women who believe strongly in personal and professional growth. She is passionate about showing women that they can be unstoppable and achieve the success they desire by stepping out of fear and unleashing their personal power.

When she is not busy spending time with her grandchildren, Michelle volunteers at local non-profit organizations in her community. It is her mission to make a difference in the lives of other women.

Chapter 23

Unleashing Your Voice

By Michelle Perkins

Who am I? That is the question I asked myself years ago as I sat there in my chair feeling numb wondering exactly who I was and what was important to me. Those three words laid heavy on my heart as I sat there trying to figure out the answer.

It was in that moment I realized I was living my life for others and not myself. For many years I let others tell me what to do or what to say both personally and professionally eventually causing my voice to become stifled. Pleasing others had become my life. My personal values and beliefs were non-existent because I indirectly took on the values and beliefs of others. I was a chameleon adapting to those around me. I no longer shared my ideas, opinions or beliefs because I had come to believe my opinion wasn't important and others would not want to hear what I had to say. I remember asking myself, "Who was I to voice my opinion? No one would listen to me." Unfortunately, the opinions of others created who I had become. A woman with no confidence, low self-esteem who felt like she wasn't good enough. The pain of feeling lost, sad and not worthy was devastating. How did I get to this point? It was then that I decided to find and share my voice with others because the world needed to hear what I had to say.

I am passionate about helping other women overcome similar obstacles in their life. Therefore, I want to share some tips that helped me discover my authentic self, allowing me to stand firm in my values and beliefs.

First, determine the things you enjoy doing in life that bring you pure joy. As you go through this process, journal what you have discovered. Then once a week, do one of those activities until you have completed all of them finding the top three that resonate with you. Those top three will reveal what is important to you and help you reconnect with your true self.

Second, pay attention to your physical and emotional state when something doesn't feel right. Whether it is who you are around or an activity you may be doing, in those moments, you are out of alignment with yourself. Taking notice of those times will prevent you from experiencing them again.

Third, stop conforming to other people's opinions and beliefs! Let go of the concern of what others think of you and start being YOU! I no longer take on the beliefs and values of others and have learned to embrace my own. I have stopped being a chameleon.

Trying to be someone you're not deprives the world of your greatness. For that reason, it has become my passion to help women discover their voice and connect with their true authentic self.

I encourage you to BE BOLD and step into your personal power by unleashing your voice. The world needs to hear what you have to say.

Melissa Porterfield

CEO

Silk Mountain

www.silkmtn.com

www.theleadershipvibe.com

www.linkedin.com/in/melissa-porterfield

https://www.instagram.com/theleadershipvibe

https://www.facebook.com/silkmntn

With over 20 years of corporate HR leadership experience, Melissa founded Silk Mountain as a consulting firm focused on helping startups design positive company cultures to attract, engage, and retain top talent, which not only drives profitability and growth, it reduces the high costs of voluntary turnover and disengagement.

In late 2020, Melissa decided to include a personal passion and created The Leadership Vibe, a coaching program that helps women develop their intuition to make confident business decisions, gain insight, and drive innovation.

In addition, Melissa is a professional speaker, has been interviewed on podcasts, radio, and television, and is also a writer. She lives in Houston with her musician husband and two dogs.

Melissa has her MEd in Educational Leadership, along with her SPHR, SHRM-SCP, Human Synergistics, and the MBTI® facilitator certifications.

Chapter 24

Your Intuition is Your Superpower!

By Melissa Porterfield

Have you ever made a decision that you regretted? A big decision that didn't work out well, the kind of decision with red flags and warning bells you chose to ignore at the time.

We **all** have intuitive abilities; they're just dormant, buried by an educational system that teaches us to focus on facts, logic and analysis to arrive at the right answer. We silence that little voice or ignore subtle feelings in our bodies. Soon we've lost touch with our innate ability to access our inner wisdom to guide our most important decisions.

The good news is that you can learn to recognize the signals that you still receive. You can learn to access your intuition at will. It's not hard and as you practice, it becomes easy. I'll teach you in four steps. In exchange, I ask that you open your mind and trust that the guidance you receive is real.

By this point, you may be wondering what kind of woo woo silliness this is and why you should listen to me. That's fair.

I've been highly intuitive my entire life and never really thought much about it. My father was in the Air Force and we moved a lot. I learned to rely on my intuition to find new friends when I started at a new school every few years.

When I started my consulting business, my intuition helped me establish solid relationships and then I noticed something alarming. I relied on my intuition with clients, but I didn't use it when I made business decisions. I had fallen into the old trap of using facts, logic and analysis. I found that I was second guessing myself, playing "what if...?" in my head and worrying that I would lose everything and end up in the street.

I noticed other women entrepreneurs I knew did the same and it occurred to me that one of my favorite Ken Blanchard quotes, "Management is a series of conversations," could be tweaked a bit "Business is a series of decisions." Just as you need to be highly skilled when having conversations as a leader, you need to be adept at making business decisions. Intuition is the key to both.

Are you ready?

1. Think about a decision you're facing. (I recommend that you start with a minor one, either personal or business-related.)

2. Find a quiet spot and place the palm of your left hand over your solar plexus- it's the area right below your ribcage where your ribs curve up to your breastbone.

3. Once your palm is in place, close your eyes and take three long, slow, deep breaths, relaxing more with each one.

4. After the third breath, focus on the sensation of your palm against your skin and notice what you feel.

Remember **don't analyze** it! Jot it down and if you find yourself questioning the experience, walk away for a bit.

My clients describe different sensations when we do this exercise the first time. I've heard "warm," "tingly," "like jumping beans," "right," and "calm," to name just a few. What I've seen is that if my clients trust the process, they know exactly what to do and they're relieved!

The same experience is accessible to you, and it is life changing. I invite you to try it, keep an open mind and watch what happens!

Maria Lobato

Owner

Just Believe Project

https://www.justbelieveproject.co.uk

https://www.facebook.com/groups/justbelieveprojectaplacetotransform

https://www.instagram.com/justbelieveproject.co.uk

https://www.facebook.com/justbelieveproject.co.uk

Author of the books "A Journey to Self-Love", "Illusion" and "Awakening", Maria Lobato has been inspiring people for many years.

A Spiritual Medium since birth, a Life and Spiritual Coach, Hypnotherapist and an NLP Master Practitioner, Maria focus her many talents helping women letting go of their past and moving into the future with confidence and self-esteem.

A big enthusiastic of Self-Development and Spiritual Awakening, Maria has gone deep inside the rabbit's hole to find herself and to heal her past, while finding her purpose in life and a strong desire to guide and assist women all over the world.

"I am someone who has been in the nitty gritty of life, just like you. But I made it through. I found my inner power, my strength, my peace, and my joy."

A positive thinker and up lifter, with a compassionate heart, Maria can't stop surprising and inspiring her many readers and supporters.

Chapter 25

I just want to be happy!

By Maria Lobato

What I am about to tell you is probably the most important thing you will ever hear. I want you to know that you are loved and cared for. Whatever challenges you have in your life right now, you are not stuck in them. I want you to know that you have value and are indeed amazing. It's ok if you don't believe me, because let's be honest, I didn't believe it either until just a few years ago.

Let me tell you a little bit about my story.

I grew up being slightly different from most children. You see, I could communicate with Spirits and that might sound pretty awesome to you right now, but to me it was scary and a shameful gift.

I kept it hidden from most people including my family and my friends. I learnt to push myself down and shut my own words for fear of judgment and disconnection. This became so ingrained in my personality that I ended up marrying a man who made me feel smaller and smaller every day.

One day I had enough and for the first time I decided "I just want to be happy".

I walked away from everything that didn't serve me, I found my voice and I learned to love myself.

Don't get me wrong, it was very hard at times. I was completely outside my comfort zone, but I persevered. I learned how to heal myself and to accept me exactly as I am. It was a jumpy but priceless ride.

This was a journey of self-discovery and empowerment. I became this vibrant woman with a voice that people actually wanted to hear. A desire started growing deep inside me to show other women that happiness is not only possible, but it is your birth right. Empowering women is my passion and it has become my life's mission.

You want to get your voice back? You want to love and express yourself showing the world how beautiful and amazing you really are? Here is what I want you to do:

1. Stop feeling sorry for yourself.

   You want to change? Decide that things will change right now. Only you have that power.

2. Allow yourself to dream.

   Set a goal, make it achievable but slightly out of your comfort zone. Fantasize and play with your dream.

3. Go for it right now.

   Don't wait for the right moment, it will never come. The moment is now. Get up and take a small action to mark your decision. Clap your hands, dance or enjoy a glass of wine knowing that simple action you are taking marks this day. It marks your decision to transform yourself into your best version. Well done!

4. Don't be afraid to ask for help.

Have a group of people you can trust to help you, even I ask for help, from friends or coaches, when I feel a bit stuck or am going through more challenging times. There is no shame, reaching out to others can be surprisingly empowering.

You got this!

Lisa Hernandez

Real Estate Advisor

The Opes Group at Compass

http://www.Lisasellsmiami.com

https://www.amazon.com/dp/B08V99F484/ref=cm_sw_r_cp_api_gl

t_Z4E4G7RTSTJ2YNEBC2JA

https://www.linkedin.com/in/lisadinonhernandez

https://instagram.com/Lisa.sells.miami

https://m.facebook.com/lisa.sells.miami

Miami real estate advisor, mom, artist, life coach and author of The Victress Journey, an 11-week series on how to pursue progress, not perfection.

Chapter 26

Pursuing Progress not Perfection

By Lisa Hernandez

In early 2010 I was married with 2 wonderful kids and I had a great career at a cruise line and lived in a decent home. Life was not always easy. My childhood was not picture perfect but overall, life was good. That summer my world turned upside down. I lost my dream job in a department wide layoff and six months later, was in the midst of a divorce. Needless to say, I struggled to find my balance. I dove into a deep depression and in December of 2012 I threw my clothes in garbage bags and left to move out of state alone. My boss at the time told me I was making a huge mistake and to turn around and go get a small apartment to figure life out. I did.

The first time I went grocery shopping I reached for milk and stopped. I was buying milk for the kids and at that moment it hit me like a ton of bricks: I had no idea who I was, what I liked, what I wanted. Over the next several years, I very painfully peeled away the layers of self-doubt, depression, anxiety and discovered this wonderful, smart, charming and brilliant woman.

During this time, I attempted to date again but after three miserable tries, I gave up in 2015 and focused on me 100%. I got my GED at 48 years old, obtained my real estate license and led the divorce group at church. I served, I gave back and realized helping others was truly the key to happiness, healing and self-worth. I refused to let my pain not be used for purpose.

I was told by many to write but I struggled with this for a very long time because I didn't have a happy ending. I was still growing and hadn't found Prince Charming to end the tale, so how was I going to end it? As I pondered this question day after day, I finally had the "aha" moment. I was pursuing perfection. Waiting for the perfect time, the perfect mate, the perfect balance in my bank account.

The other block I had was this misconception that I had to be speaking to a crowd of thousands to make a difference in the world. Guess what? The most liberating moment was accepting the fact that this journey is never ending and we never truly make "it." The golden key was understanding that pursuing perfection had led me to disappointment and so I decided to pursue progress. Life suddenly seemed magical and enjoyable. I also understood for once that not sharing my story with anyone while waiting for a mega audience was absurd. One of my ladies from my divorce group came to me, pulled me aside and told me very tearfully how I had changed her life. I smiled but deep down was in awe of her words. I got in my car and promised I would write my book and help the world one soul at a time to learn how to pursue progress, not perfection.

Kimberly Malloy

Chief Inspirational Officer

Center for Relational Health Las Vegas

http://www.malloytherapy.com

http://www.relationalhealth-lv.org

https://www.linkedin.com/in/kimberly-malloy-ms-mft-cio-69a32a48

https://www.instagram.com/relationalhealthlv

https://www.facebook.com/CRHLV

Kimberly Malloy received her Master of Science in counseling, specifically, Marriage, Family & Child Therapy and is a licensed therapist and an AAMFT Approved Supervisor with the state of Nevada in private practice. She is the founder of the Center for Relational Health LV.

The mission of CRH-LV is to inspire and develop others in relational health so they may have a positive impact on their environment. The therapy, workshops, groups, corporate retreats, and consultations are geared toward improving relationships at home, in the workplace and in the community.

Kimberly draws from her many years' experience owning a training and consultation corporation. She loves being able to help others clarify their vision, see their value and help them grow personally and professionally. Kimberly's conferences have consistently received high marks from corporations and individuals alike. Kimberly is also licensed presenter for the Color Code Personality & Character Profile and a Daring Way™ Facilitator.

Chapter 27

Time, Love, Belonging = Joy

By Kimberly Malloy

Exhausted. Tired. Angry. Isolating. Lack of Focus. Unhealthy eating or sleeping patterns. Although these can be symptoms of depression, we can experience one or all of these from time to time. Self-awareness can be the first step to walking towards wholeness. When I notice I am exhibiting behaviors of depression, the first thing I do is ask myself these questions:

Where am I spending my time?

Who am I surrounding myself with?

Do I have someone pouring into me?

Am I pouring into someone else?

Where is my JOY meter registering?

I clock out my time for a few days to see if I can identify a pattern where I am spending big chunks of time. I look at who am I communicating with, how often or sometimes, who am I avoiding? Am I allowing emotionally healthy friends and mentors to speak truth to me, or am I in a state of blaming, justifying, ignoring, or compartmentalizing? Do I have anyone I am mentoring? Am I blocking out time for them? Do I invite them to sit and watch, or come alongside me and participate in the process? Lastly, I do a temperature check on my joy, not my happiness. Happiness is situational but joy is deep. Not every day will be filled with joy but even on the hard days we can hold two emotions at the same time. I can be sad and grieving something while also finding joy in the thing that brought me grief.

When we can show up authentically, love ourselves enough to love others and receive love in return, it reminds our brain that we belong in this world. Love grows and multiplies our moments of joy.

Being a marriage and family therapist allows me to facilitate this learning process for others to improve how they show up as in their family, work and community. My joy meter is off the chart when I have the ability to work either one on one, in teams, or in group settings and do deep transformational work. I love all self-improvement work but the work I do in shame, authenticity and worthiness makes my heart bubble over with that sense of joy knowing I am making the world a better place.

Nothing brings me more joy than an attendee of my workshop or conference telling me how the work they did changed their life.

Being a certified trainer in Daring Greatly™, Rising Strong ™ Dare to Lead™, etc, which are all based on the research of Dr. Brené Brown, allows me to help individuals and organizations improve their communication, effectiveness and reduce the shame storms that often keep us stuck in unhealthy patterns. Researchers who study shame agree that keeping the negative story in our head causes the shame to grow and our joy to be non-existent. Invest in yourself and take a transformational course or try therapy to help you stay true to your values and live a joy filled life!

Donni Zheng

CEO & Health Educator

Sustainable Fashion & Health Tech Foundation

https://www.sustainable-healthy-fashion.org/fashion-revolution

https://www.linkedin.com/in/dongnizheng

https://www.instagram.com/donni_zheng

https://www.facebook.com/profile.php?id=100010004558277

Donni created a life that most people would call "exciting but seemingly impossible."

Having achieved financial freedom at the age of 25, academic excellence at the top universities UCLA and Columbia University, Donni Zheng transitioned from a science researcher to an inclusive fashion pioneer. From there, she challenges the current extreme beauty standards by leading a *Healthy Fashion Movement* with the mission of empowering women to own their bodies and achieve their full potential through media, education and life-strategy consulting.

Soon, Donni becomes one of the youngest producers at China's most influential TV network (CCTV), as well as the world's first mid-size Asian runway model, to change media's misrepresentation and eliminate body shaming. Donni also brings the most up-to-date health education to Asia to help prevent eating disorders, and provide life strategy consulting to empower women to achieve their full potential. So far, this *Healthy Fashion Movement* has inspired millions of followers from over fourteen countries worldwide.

Chapter 28

Redesign your Life: Achieve your Full Potential & Empower your Dreams

By Donni Zheng

Every day, we work our butts off. But have you noticed that after all this effort, we seem to be running in circles, and constantly dragged back by inertia? And when most of our hard work doesn't pay off, we start to feel small and incapable of achieving our dreams. And, over time we stop trying altogether. We even start persuading ourselves that those dreams are unrealistic "illusions".

So how can we do what we love, connect to our passion and achieve our full potential?

The fact is, hard work will never make up for strategic negligence. The secret to success is that when you reach a threshold, or are about to level up, your energy should immediately be redirected towards creating life strategies.

Here are a few steps to help you get started (full book coming soon!):

Step1: Identify where your passion lies to create a compass. This should be something that truly fires you up, regardless of what life throws in your face.

- Envision and redesign your ideal life like a designer: give yourself 3 ideal life options. This will protect against future bouts of self-doubt and provide the necessary room to breathe.

Step 2: Conduct a SWOT analysis of yourself: know your Strengths, be ready to convert your

- Weaknesses into assets, identify your Opportunities, and become well-prepared for your Threats.

Step 3: Incubate: train your expertise, achieve financial freedom, and manage any future risks.

- Transition from economic independence to financial freedom: the key to financial freedom is not through employment but through building our passive income.

- Don't be just a doctor, become a "visionary planner": instead of wasting energy always putting out fires and being forced to solve problems with impulsive solutions, anticipate potential problems so you can quench them before they even arise.

- Train your mind to continually run the Root-Cause analysis. Before you act, always step back, and look at the whole picture in order to see the root cause. Solve ONLY the root problem.

Step 4: Accelerate: once you have built a solid foundation from above steps, maximize your potential to achieve more with half the effort. How? It's never about your effort as an individual, but about creating synergy that works towards a mutual goal.

- Build your team.

- Create products where you can convert your one-time-effort into millions of shares.

- Amplify your impact by merging with a platform, in order to create more social value.

Step 5: Detonate: perceive any future trends, and align yourself with only the positive, irreversible ones.

- Build a Roadmap and start your Odyssey Adventure.

- Free your soul by playing an infinite game.

Doing what you love requires more than individual effort. It is born out of creating and implementing life strategies in order to break inertia, rewire your brain, flow with synergy towards your ultimate goals.

Last but not the least, always connect your passion with the needs of society to benefit as many people as possible on this special journey. Then, everything will fall into place, naturally.

Denisse Espalter

Life and Style Coach and Communications Expert

Unboxed Life and Style

http://www.unboxedlifeandstyle.com

https://www.linkedin.com/in/denisse-espalter

https://www.instagram.com/unboxed_lifeandstyle

https://www.facebook.com/unboxedlifeandstyle

Denisse Espalter is a sought-after Life & Style Coach and Communications Expert. She is also the Founder of Unboxed Life & Style; a lifestyle brand, which was created to empower women and allow them to start their journey and pivoting their mindset and self-care journey to a better version of themselves. Denisse is very passionate about what she does as she had to transform herself with big life experiences and pivot her journey!

She offers multiple courses, self-care and gifting boxes, as well as speaking events. She has a marketing and design degree as well a communications background that has led to many accomplishments, as well as working in high-level markets such as Miami, and NYC and has been featured on Dr. Oz, multiple media outlets and is now an Executive Contributor for Brainz Magazine. She is a mother of 3 beautiful girls and has learned how to successfully flourish the relationships in her now blended family with her husband.

Chapter 29

Unboxing Your Closet One Layer at a Time

By Denisse Espalter

Life can throw so many uncertainties and we need to learn how to handle our tears, our laughter, when to empower and when to walk away! The root of what can shadow our thoughts and hold us back is fear! When do we finally turn back and look at fear right in the face and say ....! Well, you can fill in the blank.

You start by unboxing the layers that hold you back and open up to what your truth is. I was there at one point. Stuck, scared and looking for some sort of affirmation that I could take a leap of faith without worrying. As women, we naturally wear different hats at different times in our lives but how far do we carry layers within that bury our true self. I know I did. I had a successful career in media & advertising helping business owners grow. Was I successful? Yes very! Was I happy? No, I felt stuck and because my subconscious was telling me that I had been there for over 8 years I had to stay because that was my career, I was too scared to walk away. I was also married with two beautiful girls! However, from the outside my marriage looked perfect, but behind closed doors it was far from that. Again, fear holding me back.

Has fear become a habit? What it comes down to is how you choose to go through life:

Is your fear greater than your faith in the unknown or is your faith in the unknown greater than your fear? I took that leap and knew that I could step into this fear and take on what I knew I deserved. I flipped that fear and knew that I wanted to look at it from my rear-view mirror.

Where am I Today? I am stronger than ever! Taking on life with a different mindset and gratitude. Stepping into the strong, loving and empowered woman that I am so proud of. Teaching my daughters to not settle and showing them that their mother is amazing, strong and the best version they have seen with much more to come! Why? Because I decided to take the steps to unbox the layers that were holding me back.

I challenge all of you to reflect on your true self. There are many ways you can practice self-reflection, however some of my favorites are the below:

- Identify your strengths and badass moments

- Start journaling

- Learn the art of gratitude

- Set specific goals

Our greatest fears are our greatest waste of time. When you focus your vision and begin to unbox what is inside, you learn to have your frequency high and move through life from a place of power and joy. Your mindset controls what you do and I ask you to identify and change behaviors that stop you from getting what you want to achieve! Remind yourself that you are a badass! You're amazing! Give yourself the permission to be you and powerful and never forget to always Love Yourself and always do it in style!

Dr. Deepali Kashyap

Deepali Kashyap, MD FACOG

Galleria Women's Health

https://galleriawomenshealth.com/

https://www.linkedin.com/in/deepali-kashyap-1b79207a/

https://www.facebook.com/galleriawomenshealth

https://www.instagram.com/galleriawomenshealth/

https://twitter.com/GalleriaWomen

Galleria Women's Health's Dr. Deepali Kashyap is Board Certified and one of the top female doctors and Gynecologists in Henderson. She has been practicing in the Las Vegas Valley since 2010.

Dr. Kashyap believes in providing individualized care for each of her patients focusing on many aspects of women's health including sexual health, abnormal pelvic bleeding, pelvic pain management, infertility, menopause management, family planning, as well as minimally invasive and major pelvic surgeries.

Dr. Kashyap is affiliated with Henderson Hospital, where she also serves on the credentialing committee. As well, she is an adjunct professor at the Touro University's school of medicine.
She completed her residency at the Beth Israel Medical Center, Albert Einstein School of Medicine in New York City.

Dr. Kashyap lives in Henderson with her husband and two children. She speaks English, Hindi and Punjabi.

Chapter 30

Doing what you love is Freedom. Loving what you do is happiness.

By Dr. Deepali Kashyap

I am a Functional Gynecologist. I help women of all ages understand and achieve true long-term health. Health not as in absence of disease but as in resilience from disease. I love what I do because I believe that for every woman I am able to help, I impact her, her family and in turn contribute towards creation of a healthier society. Nothing gives me more happiness than when my patients come back and share that they feel healthier and better than they ever have.

The year I turned 40, I started feeling changes in my own body. From a traditional medical perspective, I wasn't sick, but I knew something was not right. I had low energy, had constant migraines, always felt bloated, couldn't lose weight no matter how hard I tried and had low to no libido. No physicians I interacted with could give me an answer. All I heard was your reports are great and you are healthy. I agreed that I was not sick, but: "Was I healthy?"

I looked for answers beyond the medicine I was trained in. I researched for answers and started implementing what I found in my life.

I added and eliminated certain foods, modified behavior and lifestyle choices and focused on the psychological elements of health. Pretty soon, I started feeling "better", my migraines disappeared, had loads of energy, felt stronger and my libido improved. All the improvements happened without taking a single medicine!

Going through this myself, I also realized that a lot of my patients were going through something similar. The more I discussed these issues with my patients, the more I realized that a significant number of women had just resigned to accepting sub-optimal health as OK. I realized that many women, while suffering, had just stopped complaining. They felt that feeling the way I felt was just a normal part of their aging and that there was no hope or solution.

I was 40 years old then and I felt that unless I die in an accident or end up with a terminal illness, I probably still had another half of my life left. I want to live with a healthy mind and body and feeling my best. I also realized that many common conditions like diabetes, hypertension, osteoporosis, Alzheimer's have multifactorial causation. Genetics plays a role, but we can't underestimate the impact our lifestyle makes in causing and exaggerating these diseases. Therefore, living a certain way, eating healthy, sleeping well, exercising, maintaining optimal weight, supplementing yourself with essential vitamins, minerals can not only help manage but also prevent many of these diseases from happening. Interestingly, science also shows that we can alter genetics to some extent by making certain choices. We can chart our own course of health. That realization was a milestone for me.

My goal is to guide as many women as I can to experience what true wellness means and live a long, healthy, fulfilling and happy life, because I know that in turn would enable me to live mine.

Wendi G.

Founder/Coach/Speaker

Lighthouse Life Solutions

http://www.LinkedIn.com/in/wenditindall

https://www.instagram.com/Purpose_with_power

https://www.facebook.com/wendi.tindall

Wendi G, "The Confidence Coach," is an intuitive, empathic Certified Life Coach, Speaker, and Author. She helps professionals and entrepreneurs who want to be seen and valued, to discover REAL (Radiant, Effective, Authentic, Lasting) self-confidence, unlock their personal power, and create the life they desire.

She helps her clients get "unstuck" from that first Breakthrough Session, which is why they call her "The Unstuck Master."

With over 32 years of impassioned study of human psychology, she developed her specialized body of knowledge in "Personal Empowerment" wisdom, "Personality Profiling" mastery, and her special brand of "Confidence Coaching."

As a trusted Thought Leader, Coach and Speaker, with proven expertise in Life-skills Solutions and Relationship Breakthrough, she's been, teaching and speaking as a confidence and empowerment expert at retreats, churches, women's groups, seminars, podcasts, and other special events.

Wendi lives a powerful, purposeful, CONFIDENT life, and loves to help other women do the same!

*For a complimentary "REAL Confidence Breakthrough Session," valued at $397, email Wendi at purposewithpower@gmail.com and reference this book.

Chapter 31

Confidence Secrets Revealed

By Wendi G

You're strutting the runway like a Victoria's Secret model. You're sexy and you know it! Your confidence empowers you to live fearlessly. You can do anything.

How would you like to feel like that?!

That's how Amy Schumer's character felt in the movie, "I Feel Pretty." After a bump on the head, she "saw HERSELF" with unshakable confidence. You can have that! without the bump.

First, some bad news and some good news. The bad news: there's no magic wand and pixie fairy dust. The good news: there's a REAL solution!

I have the honor of helping amazing women, with my unique brand of 'confidence coaching to break through "stuckness," becoming all they want to be. My life is amazing, but it wasn't always this way.

I didn't become "The Confidence Coach" by accident, nor magically arrive here overnight. I was a painfully shy introvert and empath, paralyzed with insecurity, the "disease to please," and a bad case of the "not enough's." I garnered attention without trying, resulting in bullying and rejection. I felt like a misfit.

One morning in 2008, at the height of great success, I couldn't stop crying. My doctor said, "you're one drop of oil shy of frying your whole engine." That's when I began healing these wounds of my soul.

I realized, that just like Dorothy from "The Wizard of Oz," I had the power all along and so do you!

When women confidently stand in their value, they do amazing things! I'm passionate about helping women to discover REAL power and confidence.

KEY 1: You have to be YOU!

Real confidence is an inside job, not an exterior pretense. It's not extroversion, nor a personality type. It's an immovable conviction of what is TRUE about you, anchored in your soul. Then you can BE who you are, without defense, explanation, regret, or apology.

KEY 2: Address "Limiting Beliefs"

limiting beliefs inhibit your progress or potential and keep you from what you want. They're fear driven (harm, repercussion, loss, rejection). When you clean these from the windshield of your life, you'll see clearly and progress.

KEY 3: Wield the power of your CHOICE

Choice is an action you take toward or away from something, suggesting movement. When you're not moving, you're stuck.

First, recognize, not making a choice, is a choice, in reactive "default mode." (procrastination, resistance, denial, avoidance.) You're either making decisions or making excuses.

Second, there are things in life you can control and things you can't. So, choose to control what you can "proactive mode." We throw away more power than we claim.

Third, we want one giant leap for mankind, or we do nothing, but a mile is walked one step at a time. Our job is, 'get to stepping.'

Last, "Dorothy and the Scarecrow Syndrome": we don't want to make the 'wrong' decision so we do nothing. Like the movie, "Groundhogs Day," until we choose, we cannot change.

REAL confidence is obtainable. These 3 keys and many more, unlock the power you already possess but you have to leave "safe and comfortable street" and venture down a new one. Are you ready? Let's get your journey started!

Dr. Sarah Allen

Brain Gal Pediatric Neuropsychologist, Executive Director

Brain Behavior Bridge

www.brainbehaviorbridge.com

www.mybraingal.com

https://www.linkedin.com/in/sarah-levin-allen-phd

https://www.instagram/Dr.SarahLAllen

https://www.facebook.com/Brainbehaviorbridge

Dr. Sarah Levin Allen is a working mom, pediatric neuropsychologist, and parent/teacher coach. She's on a mission to help parents raise happy brains. As "The Brain Gal," she started her practice to help translate the neuroscience research to everyday life. Dr. Allen has experienced many hurdles in her life with the unexpected loss of three children, the death of her sister to breast cancer, her mother's struggles with cancer, a divorce, and a major job change.

She had to practice many of the coping strategies and self-discovery tools she taught her clients. Through these experiences, she learned that the path to happiness was in true self-understanding. Dr. Allen now uses brain tricks to help parents find themselves, their kids, and their parental values so they can create their own parent manual. As a mother and professional, she's interested in helping kids directly and supporting the people who raise their brains.

Chapter 32

It Snapped, But I Didn't

By Dr. Sarah Allen

Something strange happened to me. I was in the middle of a photo shoot for the cover of my first book. A book that's been a long time coming and one that feels like the birth of a child in a lot of ways and I turned to grab something from the corner cabinet of my kitchen and it snapped.

Not me, this time, but my bracelet. The bracelet I've been wearing on my wrist since my 28 year old sister knew she was going to die. The bracelet my sisters, mother and I put on and clasped hands for a picture, maybe our last holding hands. A bracelet that has been on my wrist for almost three years now and this time, when it snapped, I didn't.

I didn't cry, I didn't think about my sister and break down. Instead, I just held it out to my best friend. She looked at me and said, "Did that just happen?" I said, "yup." We held eyes for a brief second and then I moved on.

I didn't feel the weight, the one that has sat on my chest for years. I didn't feel crushed and drained and emotional to the point of being crippled. I just acknowledged it and I moved on.

As I sit here now, I realize the magnitude of what happened. That bracelet was chaining me to my grief. Grief over my sister, yes, but over so many things over the last few years too. When it broke, it felt like freedom. Almost like a huge relief. That weight had finally been lifted.

You see, I've spent a lot of time over the last year or so trying to find myself again. Trying to find my energy and power again. Trying to reconnect with a me that had been beaten down by life for quite some time. I realized today that I think I found her. Today was my pivot point. My moment. My "do you remember a time that changed everything for you" answer. Today, I found me and it felt damn good.

I'll never not miss my sister. As for my bracelet, I'll fix it and I'll keep it close and in a safe place. It'll always be a reminder of the beauty that was and the incredible freedom that is. From now on, I'm not looking back. I'm diving head first into the future. I'm investing in me. Look out world, here I come.

If you're like me. If you've lost yourself as an individual and as a parent. If you want your kids to grow and learn from your incredible example, I encourage you. Find yourself. Go through the steps. Use a coach as support. Do the work. It may be uncomfortable at times, actually, it will likely be uncomfortable, but embrace the discomfort. Have the tough conversations with yourself and find what makes you whole, what lights you up.

I always say that conflict breeds change. Use your conflict. Find your change. When you get to the other side, the result of the insight that you've created can change your life forever.

Melissa Bollea Rowe

SONGWRITER/OWNER

Rhyme Partners Music Publishing

www.RhymePartners.net

www.MelissaBolleaRowe.com

https://www.linkedin.com/in/melissa-bollea-rowe-4a317013

https://www.instagram.com/rhymepartners

https://www.facebook.com/rhymepartners

Melissa Bollea Rowe -Songwriter/Owner Rhyme Partners Music Publishing Founded in 2013, Rhyme Partners Music Publishing's catalog includes hundreds of cuts on both indie and major label acts with millions of combined streams on Spotify and other digital platforms. Rhyme Partners songs have been recognized, nominated for and won several independent music awards along with chart topping spins on Billboard, Music Row, Christian and Americana radio charts.

Melissa not only writes songs, publishes and performs for a living; she mentors, educates and works with individuals, corporations and organizations like The Beat Of Life, Musicians On Call and many others companies promoting awareness through the healing power of music. Melissa is the proud author of her first book "God, Gratitude & Giving. She is passionate about sharing her stories of love, success, failure, heartache, and restoration with audiences all over the world.

Contact her at mbollea@gmail.com or rhymepartners@gmail.com

Chapter 33

The Day I Cried in the Meadow

By Melissa Bollea Rowe

Recently I heard someone say, "when you feel stuck, frustrated or anxious, get out of your mind and get in your body." We know that taking a walk, riding a bike, washing the car or engaging in any physical exercise, particularly outside, makes us feel better and produces healthy endorphins. Somehow hearing it stated so simply was a beautiful reminder to me of the day I cried in the meadow.

When it comes to writing songs, I have never been short on emotional inventory. I spent years in my mind, worrying, thinking, sobbing and repeating mistakes in life. While the music I have made from the swirling of words and melodies dancing around in my head have been healing, nothing comes close to what I experienced the day I cried in the meadow.

I'm the middle child of three. My parents divorced when I was three and my mother was killed by a jealous boyfriend at thirty-three. I was filled with sadness and moved from relative to relative. I found myself trying to survive the next several decades of my life in a dark world where I could make no sense of the ungodly amount of loneliness I felt. Buried somewhere in those years, my father took his life. I often thought I may never know happiness again until the day I cried in the meadow.

I had been living, working and struggling in Nashville for 11 years. I was growing desperately tired of missing my son Chad who by this time was 28 years old and still living in Tampa, FL where he was born and where I am from. His father and I married and divorced young. Given the many broken pieces of me, I often felt I could never love again. Then on the morning of my 47th birthday I got an email that changed my life in a single sentence, "Hi Missy, sometimes I wonder, how are you" that ultimately led me to the day I cried in the meadow.

The message was from my first crush, Sean Patrick Rowe. We fell in love as children in 7th grade. We remained friends for years until life sent us down separate roads. The last card I wrote him 25 years earlier, read "Hi Sean, sometimes I wonder, how are you?" We are now happily married. Of all the breathtaking places my husband has taken me to nothing stands out as much as the day we hiked into Horseshoe Meadow, located in the high terrain of the Southern Sierra Nevada Mountains in California. The air was clear, the sun was shining, the wild flowers were in full bloom and it was there that I felt heaven wrap its arms around me. I had no choice but to weep, to be in my body. Since then, I have found that a walk in nature walks the soul back home.

Whatever you do, I encourage you to stay connected to nature, to your loved ones. Make a list of what you desire your days to look like and what they currently look like. Begin to adjust accordingly. Today my son lives close to me, my career and life are thriving. I am forever grateful to this journey and the day I cried in the meadow.

Lynda Bowers

Broker/Owner

ProEdge Realty, LLC

www.ProEdge.Pro

www.LyndaBowersTrustee.com

https://www.linkedin.com/in/lynda-bowers-7927a73

https://www.instagram.com/bowers.lynda

https://www.facebook.com/lynda.bowers.90

Describing Lynda Bowers' childhood as abusive is a masterpiece of understatement. Lynda was always on the edge, primed to perceive threat and anticipate pain. Despite adversities at home, old-order Mennonite neighbors often took her in and served as her angels. They taught her the value of helping others. They made her feel strong and safe when her home life gave neither. They taught her that God uses ordinary women to do extraordinary things. And as a young adult with a passion to overcome, Lynda set out to do just that, taking advantage of every opportunity.

Aged 17, a police dispatcher by night and college student by day, Lynda began achieving an excellent education including three years post graduate work at the Kent State University Center for Public Administration and Public Policy and being accepted as a participant in the Harvard Law School Negotiation and Mediation Project with Author and Professor, Roger Fisher.

Today, Lynda uses those early life lessons maintaining success as the Broker/Owner of ProEdge Realty, serving her community as an elected Township Trustee for more than two decades and holding leadership positions in numerous civic and charitable organizations.

Chapter 34

From Abuse and Violence to Success and Inspiration

By Lynda Bowers

Beyond nurturing faith, growing up in an old-order Mennonite environment, developed in me a personal responsibility in service to others and to myself. I realized I am not a product of what happened to me, but how I reacted to it. I learned positivity is a choice, the power is ours. Opportunities to help others in the community showed me that happiness in our lives depends on the quality of our own thoughts and goals. Those early life lessons are my most treasured.

By age 30, I had moved up to working in the city law department. To make a little extra money, I got a real estate license. Because I was working a full-time job, my broker didn't expect much.

Those early life lessons fueled success in my real estate career. Doing the little things right. Understanding the importance of building relationships. Finishing what you start. My real estate business took off in a way I could never have imagined and I loved it but I struggled toward the holy grail of "balance" barely hitting an occasional harmony. Still, I often dreamed of what the leap into Real Estate full-time could look like. The vision was a job that I loved while also affording me the time to be involved in my community and charities, the underpinnings of my youth

I longed for, those things that kept me sane and safe when my home environment was anything but.

I wanted desperately to take that leap but like so many other women, I was waiting for that perfect moment. Guess what? There is NO perfect moment. A business owner in my community who I was blessed to call a friend, made an out of nowhere comment to me one day. She said "We all deserve a job we love, a life filled with fun and purpose. You haven't even begun to tap your potential to leave things better than you find them." Facing some major changes in my personal life at that time, it was absolutely the WORST time to consider a professional change but I had strong faith. God planted the seed and I became determined to grow it.

I took the leap and have never looked back. I have an amazing business and a wonderfully fulfilling life. The business success allows me both the time and opportunity to serve my community and neighbors. I am blessed to hold leadership positions supporting several charities, including one that serves children in distress.

I can't spin all the plates at once but I thrive on having them all up in the air. If you are reading this book, you are likely a woman like me, driven, full of energy and with lots of goals. Today is full of opportunity, start the change now. Decide what lights you up and do whatever it takes to make it happen and when you make it happen. Pay it forward!

Cecilia Duffy

Doctor of Chiropractic/Owner

Geneva Chiropractic Clinic

https://www.genevachiro.wixsite.com/genevachiropractic

https://www.facebook.com/genevachiropractic

Cecilia Duffy

Dr. Cecilia Duffy is a chiropractor with a post-graduate specialty in Applied Kinesiology, owner of Geneva Chiropractic Clinic in Geneva, Ohio, and in practice since 1986. Her passion is to serve her patients and assist them in attaining their best possible health, physically and emotionally, through natural therapies, nutrition, and supplementation. She is in general practice seeing a wide variety of ailments from musculoskeletal pain and injuries to hormone imbalances, gut issues, and overall wellness care. She provides gentle chiropractic treatment and a holistic approach to her patient's health concerns.

Dr. Duffy taught on a post-graduate level for six years before committing to devote her time to her practice and being mom to an awesome daughter. Away from her clinic, she serves on non-profit groups that support the arts in her community, working women, and scholarships for young ladies attending college. For fun, she loves to take adventures and paint and hide rocks.

Chapter 35

You're Never Done Growing

By Cecilia Duffy

Imagine you're a woman in her prime: forty-one, running a business, managing a household and raising a child. Both you and your mother are diagnosed with breast cancer within months of each other and you're watching your mother die while you begin to recover.

Welcome to my 2004. Talk about a wake-up call.

My training as a chiropractor taught me that all human ailments stem from alterations in your structural, chemical, or emotional health. Here I am, a chiropractor practicing what she preaches taking care of my physical body, a healthy diet and I get *this*?

Growing up, I worked in my father's chiropractic clinic and learned how to manage the clinic and care for patients. Our relationship was complicated. I was emotionally neglected by him unless I was actively doing something that pleased him or made him look good. I remember there being a subtle grooming and coercion to become a chiropractor and I learned that whenever I mentioned becoming a chiropractor, I received his attention. I took these small bits of attention and filled the gaping hole where his fatherly love should have been. I chose to go into chiropractic, but my choice was made for the wrong reasons.

Upon joining him in his practice after college, there was a constant low-level friction in the clinic that would erupt periodically in the form of him shaming me and trying to control "how things should be done." Even after spending my adult life trying to please him, I was not enough in his eyes and I believed myself to be a second-rate doctor because I chose to approach my patients care in a different way.

Flash forward. I had reached a breaking point from the stress of my own illness and the death of my mother. As I began to heal my physical body from cancer, it was time for me to attend to my neglected emotional health.

I started counseling and unleashed Pandora's box. Though it was exhausting, I learned about my childhood emotional traumas and how they influenced my choices as an adult. I relived my breast cancer, my mother's death, my father's treatment of me, the premature death of my husband and estrangement from my siblings. I was devastated that I was eighteen years into a career that I thought I loved only to realize that I was emotionally manipulated into choosing it. I had to allow myself to fully feel and wallow in newfound negative emotion that I had repressed for so long and then see what meaning I could derive from the suffering I had experienced.

I now believe that the experiences in my life brought me opportunity for growth. Because I ignored them for so long, these growth opportunities came back stronger until I let them in. After my emotional awakening, my lesson is this: I no longer live to please others. I have a newfound sense of ownership in my life and career choices moving forward.

This growth has given me a huge change in perspective. Even after a crisis of faith over my career, I realized that I do actually love what I do. It only causes me more pain to wish things in my past were different and I have found peace by accepting my history just the way it was, not how I wish it would have been.

What I am working on now? Treating myself with the same love, grace and compassion that I have given to my patients all along. I hope you take this as a reminder to do the same.

Evelyn Gandrup

Owner/Mentor/Coach

eGandrup AB – Women's Empowerment

www.egandrup.com

https://www.linkedin.com/in/evelyn-gandrup-32076a18

https://www.instagram.com/egandrup

https://www.facebook.com/evelyn.gandrup

Evelyn has worked as an entrepreneur for more than 20 years. She sold her business a few years ago, a wine import, and started a new career. Today Evelyn helps women dream big and bold and help them find the courage to change their life circumstances to live their dream—having made the journey herself.

Evelyn is a professional coach ACC, a certified Theta Healer, holds a Bachelor degree in Project Management within Publishing and is a certified wine sommelier. She has 20+ years of entrepreneurial experience. Evelyn works as chairman of the board in a Housing Cooperative. She serves as Consul at InterNations, a worldwide ex-pat organization. She mentors teenagers through Mentor, a non-profit organization.

Evelyn is an avid reader, writes poetry, does bouldering, yoga and meditate. She loves travelling the world. She loves to be part of the women empowerment movement and change the world one step at a time.

Evelyn resides in Sweden but works internationally.

Chapter 36

The Power of You

By Evelyn Gandrup

I didn't have a dream or a role model when growing up. No one talked about dreams or visions and there were no engaging discussions or talk about feelings. Silence was queen and the culture of my home. The silence and the fact that I was told to keep my opinions to myself made me a very insecure child.

The great tragedy that formed my life hit when I was 17 years old. My father died after three years of fighting cancer and the family couldn't cope with the loss and the world became a solid black ocean of anxiety, grief and loneliness. Eventually, we fell apart.

Even before my father died, I had the feeling of not belonging, not being in the right place, being lost. This feeling followed me into my adult life.

Yet, I've lived a successful life on the outside, surrounded by my family and friends, running my own business and travelling the world but not being truly happy. Something was missing. I felt detached, not being in contact with me and my feelings. I realized the significance of being a total stranger to myself.

One day, in midlife, I finally found the courage to change everything. I sold my business, divorced my husband of 25 years, moved to another city and started the process of finding out who I am and what I want.

My inner journey was the most exciting and rewarding experience yet. I went on a terrifying roller-coaster adventure and met my worst fears and out of this world grief but also love and relief. I broke free from my limitations and discovered that I was a moon in the wrong galaxy. There was never anything wrong with me, but I was just not able to shine in the environment I had been living. When finding my own space, I also found my voice and dream.

This realization is what I love to share.

It took time for me to understand that I am a powerful woman, 55 years to be exact. It is never too late to find your voice, your spark, your magic. I love to guide women so they can shorten the timeline in finding and living their dream life.

I use my life journey as inspiration and power to help women find out what they really want and be courageous in dreaming big and bold. You need to be unapologetic about your greatness and make the changes you need to reach your vision. Ask yourself what you really want. We are all on a timeline and we waste so much time doing things we don't like and spend time in all the wrong places. You need to live life by design, YOUR design.

My dream for us collectively as powerful women is to live OUR DREAM, live the life WE choose and become outstanding role models for young girls who need to know that their voice matters. I believe this is our obligation, to show them we can live our dream so they can. This is my current life and mission and it makes me happy.

Isa O'Hara

OWNER

Wealth by Design™

www.isaohara.com

https://www.linkedin.com/in/isa-ohara-2802631

https://www.instagram.com/isa.ohara

https://www.facebook.com/ohara.isa

Isa O'Hara is a single mom of two young men. She earned a degree in Computer Science (before the internet) and enjoyed her time in the Information Technology field for over 20 years. When things became more corporate, Isa found the strictness to be stifling and decided to do what ALL I.T. people do – open an organic coffee shop. It promoted local business, local artists, and provided real food. In doing this, Isa discovered that she really didn't love the "brick and mortar" business model and sold the coffee shop to pursue a home-based business, which gave her the freedom she needed to do the things she truly loved.

Isa has a life from which she never needs a break – which led her to create her program: Wealth by Design™, which is designed to help women create the next level of wealth in all areas of their life.

Chapter 37

Wealth by Design™: Create Extraordinary Abundance on your Terms

By Isa O'Hara

I wake up when I'm done sleeping. I have 100% control over my schedule. I give my time and money to the causes and people that matter to me. I truly love my life.

My life wasn't always like this. I had a corporate job in the Information Technology field (translate to "computer nerd"), I had a great house, kids in private school, I volunteered at my school and church and my partner and I brought in a nice income. I became disenchanted with corporate life because it didn't feed my free-spirit. So I gave it up in order to find "freedom" by starting up an organic coffee shop because that's what ALL I.T. people do.

I quickly found that while my coffee shop connected me with some great people and it provided amazing organic coffee and real food while supporting local farmers, businesses and artists it was not quite "the dream." It was closer than my corporate gig but not quite there. In the middle of owning the coffee shop, my marriage ended as well. Which left me with $164,000 of debt that did not include the house or the land that we owned. That was another ½ million on top of that. To say my life was "stressful" didn't even scratch the surface.

Something had to change:

1. I had to take full responsibility for where I was. From there I had to be able to SEE what was possible, to find my heart's desire. To really feel into what I wanted my life to look like and how I wanted to feel living in my life.

2. I had to change my thought patterns. I had to learn to really BELIEVE it, inside every cell of my body down to the DNA..

3. I had to create a plan to get where I needed to go. I had to figure out how to pay off the debt and then once that was done then the next step and the next.

4. Finally, I had to refine my plan. Since paying off $164,000 in debt took a little time, my initial thoughts about what I wanted to be, have and do also morphed along the way, they grew bigger. Most important, I had to keep my eye on the prize and not let my ego take me away from living my best life. The life I had designed.

I was able to sell my coffee shop to pursue a home-based business I started working on while owning the shop, which gave me more time to spend with the people who mattered to me as well as spending time volunteering to help the people really looking to have a better life and to travel so I could experience different parts of the world and learn about different cultures.

You are probably at a point where you know you want something more. You've already figured out how to have a comfortable life. You've figured out how to donate your time to causes you care about. Now is the time to move into the next level. To really find your dream.

Kathleen Carozza

Author/Advisor

Silvia Gupta Coaching

https://www.instagram.com/Carozza_katejr

https://www.facebook.com/kate.carozza.5

Kathleen Carozza was born and raised near the Finger Lakes Region of Upstate New York before being drawn to the warm weather and job opportunities of Atlanta, Georgia in the early 1990s.

Beyond her almost 30-year career, her top three interests include teaching, amateur photography, and traveling.

Recent highlights that combined all three were teaching at international academies in Hungary, Thailand, and El Salvador, then traveling the beautiful countryside's.

Chapter 38

Life's Purpose

By Kathleen Carozza

I don't think it is an understatement to say that God gave me a miracle. He had a conversation with me in which I instantly understood life's purpose. Within this conversation, He charged me to decipher and then write about the ingredients of life's purpose. My dilemma, how to translate the feeling given to me into words powerful enough to cause people to reflect. In this reflection, people *can* see truth.

I took a leap of faith and wrote the book, which really wasn't that much of a leap after the miracle I had just received. My leap was inspired by my innate knowing that the information required would be provided to me somehow or some way. Little did I know that the eight-month process I went through to amass the information for the book was actually the same template or process for finding your purpose.

During this time, patterns emerged and I realized I could articulate the ingredients and define a step-by-step process for people to find their life's purpose and even create an income with it. This process includes, what appear to be, the common ingredients of:

Thoughts

Emotions

Beliefs

Actions

Reactions

Awareness

Energy

Mental faculties

Universal Laws

These simple ingredients become the magic of creation with a little understanding and a lot of experimenting. I've learned that they are only common or dormant when you don't understand how they work interconnectedly. Most of us have been conditioned to view life as reactionary. I understood that He wants us to be proactive and follow our guidance or intuition to experience so much more. All of these ingredients are at your disposal every day to concoct any variation of life that makes you happy, which brings me to the purpose of life.

Some people feel as if they haven't found or discovered their purpose in life while others found it and are thriving. Entertain this thought for a second, the purpose of life is simply to be happy. That's it. Nothing more, nothing less. Let me say that again. Your purpose in life is to be happy. How you choose to be happy is free will and it resets every second of every day. Feel it, follow it and thrive with it.

All the limitations you began to hear in your head as you read that last sentence are expectations that society has conditioned you with, period. That's what's holding you back.

How do you find purpose/happiness? You need to feel alignment. Quiet yourself to hear the deeper, softer voice. This is your guidance system to happiness and also your template to create any income you desire.

Want to know more? What excited thought did you have right then? Follow your intuition. Where this chapter ends, is where your guidance must pick up. Slow down, be present and feel what you are supposed to do next. Trust that intuition leads you to your purpose. It is never wrong.

Lara Desir

OWNER

Desir Immigration

https://www.desirimmigration.com

https://www.linkedin.com/in/desir-immigration-3565ba206

https://www.instagram.com/desirimmigration

https://www.facebook.com/desirimmigration

Lara Desir is an ambitious and soft hearted mother of three who traveled to Canada in June of 1999. She always had a passion for helping others. She worked for a couple weight loss companies as a weight loss counselor, which she enjoyed very much. Thereafter, she wrote her first book "Not the Typical Weight Loss Book".

Lara had tried and failed at business ventures and accomplished a small success in her final network marketing gig. A few years before completing her MBA online while pregnant with her last baby, Lara a single mother at the time, completed her Ontario high school diploma while enrolled full time in her undergraduate program. In the past she helped several family members and friends get positive outcomes with their immigration applications, which lead to her eventual decision to create a fulfilling career as a licensed Immigration Practitioner.

Chapter 39

Dreams of a Small Island Girl

By Lara Desir

"You were too busy making babies" he said while he seemed to judge me for living in a small one bedroom basement at the time, as a single mother with my two young daughters, not knowing the heartache that I had just been through. Those words pierced through my DNA and awakened a burning desire for me to achieve great success in life, to leave a legacy for my children, to take care of my family and to make a difference in the world.

I will go more into depth about this life altering "disparaging blessing" in my next book "A foreigner myself". At 29 years old, after that comment, I immediately made the decision to attend university. I also decided to become an entrepreneur, so I opened up a small children's clothing store named "Bella's Place" after my youngest daughter Isabella. That Business failed so I started a Temp agency, which also failed, among other businesses. I did eventually have some success in my final one, a natural health alternative company, primarily because of my belief in the product as it helped my father control his high blood pressure.

"Aren't you too old to go back to school?" This was the question that my beloved aunt asked me when I excitedly told her that I had planned on applying to get into University. Those words made me want to succeed even more, as well as to prove her wrong. So I completed the prerequisite courses, got accepted into a couple universities and relocated over 60 miles away from my loved ones. Luckily, I did not back down from my decision to go back to school, as a university degree was a prerequisite for completing the post graduate Immigration Practitioner program. After helping several people achieve positive results with their immigration processes, today I now have my own practice (Desir Immigration) after a long struggle with trying to get licensed. If I can achieve the level of success that I have despite my struggles and circumstances, then any woman can.

Many women out there, whether they are single or married, young or senior, can end up in situations where they struggle to get ahead and everything they do never seems to work, however the best thing that any woman (or man) can do for themselves in order to achieve their dreams is to first have a positive mindset. Decide what you want to do, write it down, write down everything that you need to do in order to achieve this goal. Obsess about that goal and put all or most of your energy into achieving this goal. Do not create a backup plan as this could affect your mentality and you may not push as hard to achieve that goal. Even though it seems impossible, DO NOT GIVE UP! You will achieve your dreams.

Sherry Scott

Certified Holistic Nutrition Consultant

Isagenix International

https://www.sherryscott.isagenix.com

https://www.linkedin.com/in/sherry-scott

https://www.instagram.com/sndscott78

https://www.facebook.com/voicetruth

Sherry Scott is a Certified Holistic Nutrition Consultant, working in the Health and Wellness industry. She provides nutritional guidance through super-food nutrition and Nobel prize- winning science for anti-aging at the cellular level. She believes while we are living longer, we are not living healthier. Sherry has a passion to help clients live their healthiest lives now.

Sherry's background and education is in Human Resource management in high tech manufacturing, bio tech, and non-profit, serving in the local church in both Human Resources and Women's Ministry.

Blessed to be married with two grown sons, Sherry is a very proud grandmother. She resides in North Las Vegas.

Chapter 40

Why Do Hard Things?

By Sherry Scott

In this chapter, I will share experiences that taught me valuable life lessons. My hope is that you will find some encouragement and inspiration for your journey. Regardless of where you are on your journey, I am going to challenge you to do some hard things.

As a young woman I landed a job at the US Embassy in London. I grew up in Atlanta. My family rarely traveled beyond Daytona Beach or the Smoky Mountains. When I announced to my family that I had signed a government contract and was moving to London for two years, their expressions were one of "she's going to fall off the planet." I will admit, I knew no one in London. A telephone interview, an in-depth background check and a few weeks later I met my boss and his wife at Heathrow airport! Call it the inexperience of youth, but I was not afraid, I had stars in my eyes! The experience was unforgettable! I traveled all over Europe and that was great, but the opportunity to work in an American Embassy with top State Department officials, attend prestigious English events, serve on Secretary of State visits gave me up close exposure to the diplomatic core and another part of the world. I gained needed confidence and poise. I learned I could hold my own in that environment. Sometimes we do not know what we need until we experience it. Moving to another country where you know no one could be a pretty hard thing for some. I did not even know what the diplomatic service was when I said yes. Had I been afraid to take the risk, I would have missed so much! My wish for you is to be *open* to do hard things.

My career was in Human Resource management in several industries. One of my favorites was working in non-profit, the local church. I was HR Director working for the lead pastor in a mid-sized church when the church decided to make a movie, a full-length, faith-based film. I was asked to be the Catering Team Manager and oh yes, there was no budget! I simply trusted if they thought I could do it, then I would do it. I knew nothing about the film industry or catering, but I knew the people of the church well and I told myself that this was not my sole responsibility. So, I built a team and pretty much gave my life over to the movie for 9 weeks. The movie was a great success and shown all over the United States and abroad. I was tested every day, but I learned *the importance of unity, the power of trust and the love of team.* Food is super important on film crews. If you do not feed the crew, production halts, money is lost and no one is happy. I prayed every day for the unity of my team. I learned the value of collaboration with all types of people, total novices like me and professional actors, directors and producers. Ladies, collaboration is such a needed skill in life and business.

I reflect on opportunities like the ones shared above as once in a lifetime experiences. How do you decide to take on something big without any experience? I cannot answer for you, but here are some things you will want to think about.

- How does your heart feel about the project? Is this a heart thing and are your emotionally connected to it in a positive way?

- Will the project benefit others? Is it bigger than you and does it excite you?

- Would you do this even if it paid nothing? My first movie project paid nothing, but I worked on two other movies and the third one paid well!

Sometimes opportunities come quick and you may not have a lot of time to think about it. They could turn out to be *your* opportunities of a lifetime by awakening *your passion and fire within*. I do not want you to miss that. Be brave, take risks, for nothing can substitute for experience.

Today, I work in health and wellness. I am super passionate about holistic nutrition and helping people live their healthiest lives now.

Queashar Halliburton

CEO

Queashar Detroit Publishing, LLC

https://www.sharhalliburton.com

https://www.linkedin.com/in/queasharhalliburton

https://www.instagram.com/qdpublishing

https://www.facebook.com/qdpublishing

Although many abandon their goals and dreams because of fear, uncertainty, procrastination, she turns each of those things into stepping-stones to her success. For Queashar L. Halliburton, CEO and founder of Queashar Detroit Publishing, LLC, her greatest success to date resulted from living outside the box and operating in her God-given gifts and purpose. As an international best-selling author, certified success coach, and professional speaker, Queashar empowers professionals to push past self-sabotaging behaviors and utilize their innate abilities to excel in life and business.

Queashar is a graduate of Les Brown's Power Voice System for speakers and coaches. She has been featured in Times Square, FOX, CBS, NBC, Speakers Magazine, and Courageous Woman Magazine. Queashar is also contributing writer for Advance Magazine, Publish Magazine, and the author of Skyrocket Your Success! 10 Keys to Refocus, Reposition & Reclaim Your Purpose!

Chapter 41

Unmasking the Imposter & Seizing Your Seat at the Table!

By Queashar L. Halliburton

Imposter Syndrome makes you feel like you are not good enough. It makes you feel as if you are subpar and you are not qualified to have a seat at the table. The inferiority complex may be a symptom of something from your past that has not been addressed. Most times, this feeling may stem from something from our childhood. It may have been something that someone you cared about said to you when you were a little girl. That negativity planted a seed of doubt and you watered it, nurtured it and gave it some sunlight. Now that seed of doubt has caused you to procrastinate.

I know about Imposter Syndrome because I like 70% of people, suffered from this self-debilitating mindset for years (Forbes.com). I had the education, experience, training, and ability, but I kept procrastinating. I thought everything had to be perfect for me to leap into my calling. I waited for years to accomplish personal goals.

Let's cut to the chase and ask the million-dollar question! How do you manage Imposter Syndrome? To be honest, you must check that feeling of inferiority at the door! Just like you check your coat at the door of a fine dining establishment. All seats at the table have already been reserved and guess what? Your name has been reserved!

When I reference "The Table" I mean, the office, the conference, that speaking engagement you are afraid to apply for, that upper management job, that collaboration project, entrepreneurship, writing that book, whatever that next level elevation shift is for you.

Here are three ways to unmask the Imposter Syndrome and seize your seat at the table!

1. Release the idea that everything must be perfect before you leap into your purpose. Everything cannot be perfect, start where you are. You will perfect your craft as you grow. Practice makes perfect.

2. Reaffirm your qualifications by taking an accurate inventory of your accomplishments. List 10 things that you have accomplished professionally and personally in the past five years. Update your resume. A few years ago, I updated my resume and looking at all my accomplishments was empowering! I had proof of my accomplishments in a professional format.

3. Get rid of the negative mindset. Retrain your brain to think positively. Do daily exercises to reverse your negative thinking. Just like you physically train for a marathon, you must intentionally retrain your brain to think positively!

Try this exercise to retrain your brain. When you get a negative thought that makes you feel like you are unqualified to have a seat at the table, envision that you are introducing yourself to a new colleague using a power affirmation. For example, you could say, "Hello, I am Queashar L. Halliburton. I am a powerful woman of faith and purpose. I am worthy of this seat at the table! My God-given gifts have led me to this position and I belong here!" *(Insert your name.) You have earned a seat at the table. You are just as brilliant as the person you are sitting next to and don't you ever forget that!

Liane Haynes-Smith

Founder

DreamsEnvision

www.DreamsEnvisions.com

www.LHSDreamsEnvisions.com

www.instagram.com/dreamsenvisions

www.facebook.com/dreamsenvisions

Liane Haynes Smith is a Transformational Life Coach. For over 20 years, Liane has been studying and implementing transformational success principles as a corporate leader of highly successful sales & service teams and in her role as a coach for individuals and groups. She is the founder of DreamsEnvisions, a relational coaching program focused on guiding individuals to find their version of soul-satisfying success, expanding perceptions and boundaries, as well as finding joy in each day.

When Liane is not coaching and teaching workshops, her favorite activity is exploring Los Angeles with her husband of 27 years, proudly watching her Daughter take on life as a young adult, and keeping her two loveable canines out of mischief. Regular engagements with a group of long-term friends, she classifies as the Tribe, combined with renovating a 1937 English cottage, and travel also fit into the equation that is Liane's life.

Chapter 42

Forward Thinking Present Mindfulness

By Liane Haynes-Smith

Having a life plan and setting goals is key to our overall success. By blueprinting our future, we are putting in motion actions that reflect our passions and expectations for ourselves. Implementing our life map will require hard work and discipline, but the advantages can promote a meaningful life of value, fulfillment and happiness. At the beginning of our quest, it is essential to maintain a sense of the present as we journey into our future.

Great excitement comes from knowing where we want to go. This feeling, combined with determining how to actualize our desires, can give one a sense of expansiveness and greater power over life circumstances. While all our faculties are focusing on reaching our desired goals, this may be a perfect time to pause and acknowledge the person we are in the moment. As we are working on our goals, continue to chart the transformation that comes with self-mastery and develop new behaviors and skills. While moving forward, enjoy the journey and pause to relish the gifts that come with everyday living.

There was a time in my life in which my career trajectory ended and it was time to re-calibrate who I was and what I wanted to achieve. The closing of one door highlighted a dream that had been poking at my consciousness for some time. This shift in life allowed me to look at my neglected desire with new interest. Within days I had a plan and with laser precision, my full attention became focused on a new destination. I revved up my engines and directed all of my energy on a specific set of goals. I was barreling down the highway at 100 miles an hour with a new career in view. Until one day, I hit a snag that temporarily forced me to change gears and slow down. Altering my pace was both disappointing and frustrating. While I was having a private pity party, I heard the laughter of a child who was walking underneath my office window. The sound of young laughter was so sweet to my ears. I realized that I had become too absorbed in what was waiting for me in the future. I had disengaged from the delight of everyday living. Goals and a bright future are essential but failing to pause each day and take in the beauty of life are significant.

As a Transformational Life Coach, my passion is empowering people to bring their dreams into a place of reality by way of specific and attainable goals. Concurrent with one on one sessions and providing courses of study, I encourage Clients to pay attention to who they become on the journey. I also emphasize that no matter what one is going through or how hard it is, there can be joy. Listening to the sound of children's laughter, the smell of something baking, a beautiful cloud formation in the sky are all reasons for intertwining our present with our future.

For maintaining a balance between your future and the present, consider these rituals.

Utilize a journal to include the following:

- Record your feelings and notate wins and opportunities.

- Each day list five reasons to be grateful.

- Build a list of what inspires you to feel joy and engage in a joyful activity when your spirit needs a lift.

Making our journey a blend of forward thinking and present mindfulness ensures that we live rich, abundant lives to the fullest.

Deborah McDaniel

Owner

The Girl Can Write!

www.thegirlcanwrite.com

www.deborahjmcdaniel.com

https://www.linkedin.com/in/deborahjmcdaniel

www.instagram.com/debcanwrite

www.facebook.com/debcanwrite

Deborah is the owner of The Girl Can Write!, a ghostwriting, and editing agency for spiritual and transformational coaches, consultants, and entrepreneurs. She specializes in helping thought leaders get their groundbreaking ideas out of their heads using a collaborative interview-based writing model to allow thoughts to freely flow while allowing time to work through mental blocks.

In addition, she is an intuitive mindset & strategy coach for new and aspiring freelance creatives. Through her coaching services, she guides and mentors new and aspiring freelance creatives to develop confidence and trust in themselves and empowers them to create a soul-aligned strategy to grow their authentic online presence without fear of being judged, rejected, or feeling burnt out.

Deborah's mission is to inspire stressed, burnt-out 9 to 5 moms that they can create a comfortable, flexible, and abundant life working for themselves as a freelancer or blogger, even without having prior experience.

Chapter 43

When the Universe gives you a nudge . . .

By Deborah McDaniel

Three years ago, while 7 months pregnant with my third child, I suffered a complete mental breakdown. Looking back, what I thought was the moment when my life fell apart, was actually the moment I woke up and decided to live for me. Up until that point, unknowingly, I lived for everyone else.

I remember the first moment I felt like it was my job to be the peacekeeper for everyone. I was six years old, watching my parents violently fight and thinking, *this is all my fault. I didn't follow the rules and now mom and dad are going to kill each other!* In that moment, unbeknownst to me, I made a vow that I would always follow the rules to keep the peace and that has always been my north star, my guiding voice.

Though my heart constantly yearned to be in service of others, to impact and inspire people to follow their dreams, I spent all of my twenties and first half of my thirties doing the things that others expected of me. I went into Corporate America, bouncing around from job to job as I tried to scale the corporate ladder.

On the outside, I looked successful and in some ways, I was. I had a nice salary, nice title and TONS of responsibility. I was miserable because each victory required a sacrifice. Piece by piece, as I gained more success in my career, my life began to shatter. My marriage was falling apart and the amount of work I had on my plate kept me physically present but mentally absent from my kids' lives. The sacrifices kept building and building until it felt like I no longer existed outside of my job. I was a shell of myself. Strong, ambitious and confident on the outside, but completely crumbled on the inside.

Eventually, my shell cracked and through those cracks the real me, the person who had been hiding in the shadows and waiting, spoke up. The person who never wanted to work in corporate and instead wanted to help change the world spoke up and I was grateful to hear from her.

That's how I embraced the next phase of my career as a ghostwriter and editor. In six months of starting this business, I made over $30,000, while only soliciting on UpWork. I now mentor others on creating a successful and profitable freelance business.

Making the shift from doing what was expected of me to doing what I love has been the most terrifying and FULFILLING experience I've ever had and I wouldn't trade it for the world.

My hope for you, as you read this chapter, is to know that you deserve to go after your dreams and the only person standing in your way, is you. You can achieve anything you want, as long as it is rooted in passion and purpose.

Dr. Gina Nick

Naturopathic Physician

www.drgina.com

www.blog.drgina.com

https://www.linkedin.com/in/drginanick

https://www.instagram.com/drginanick

https://www.facebook.com/drginahealing

Dr. Gina Nick, NMD, PhD is a world-renowned Naturopathic Physician, educator, researcher, and product formulator based in Newport Beach, California.

She has been named a "top celebrity doctor" to A-list celebrities and professional athletes worldwide. She is also considered a thought leader in her field for the treatment of autoimmune diseases, inflammation, addiction recovery, depression, anxiety, fatigue, weight gain, and sexual dysfunction. Dr. Gina is a partner with actress Suzanne Sommers' Forever Health Network.

Most recently, Dr. Gina was named among Marquis Who's Who Top Doctors Honors Edition dedicated to the first responders of COVID-19.

At the age of 23, Dr. Gina graduated from medical school, where she became the first Director of Research for the world's top supplement company. With her wealth of knowledge and supplement expertise, she was invited to present her findings at NASA's Johnson Space Center in Houston, TX. She has been featured on lifestyle television shows, podcasts and has made many personal appearances. She also presents her work on glutathione at medical conferences throughout the world.

Dr. Gina is the Executive Healthcare Consultant to Local and Government Agencies, President Emeritus of the California Naturopathic Doctors Association, and Founder and Director of HealthBridge in Newport Beach, California, named "Top Medical Practice 2017".

In 2020, Dr. Gina launched Apothicaire By Dr. Gina, her own brand of high-quality nutritional supplements.

Dr. Gina is a published author, entrepreneur, mother, and television personality, featured on The List, Discovery, HGTV and PBS. She is licensed to practice medicine in both California and Hawaii and is also a certified yoga instructor.

Chapter 44

Building the Bridge to a New Type of Medicine

By Dr. Gina Nick

"There are no heartbeats." The words no expectant mother wants to hear. It was November 11th, 1998, the day I learned my unborn twins were not viable. It was the most painful day of my life, and the beginning of my medical journey. I was newly married, fresh out of naturopathic medical school and pregnant. I asked an obstetrics professor, also a certified midwife, to manage the pregnancy. I had faith in her abilities. A month later, I woke up and intuitively knew I was having twins. Little did I know I would encounter pregnancy problems. I found out there was no heartbeat on either fetus. This was devastating. For the next 13 years, I had repeated miscarriages. It was soul-crushing. No one in the naturopathic profession could explain why this was happening. Then, in September of 2011 at the age of thirty-nine, I was invited to lecture on managing thyroid disorders. While preparing for the lecture, I found a study that discussed the importance of testing thyroid function during the 6-8 week window of a pregnancy. It stated that patients with recurring miscarriages who have a significant elevation in TSH levels should be treated promptly. Inspired by that information, I selected a qualified physician who discovered my TSH level had skyrocketed to 11! This was an alarming number and thankfully I was successfully treated. It was an unforgettable experience that ultimately altered the way I practice medicine. Months later, I was full-term at the birthing center. During my last visit, I asked the midwife about their emergency transport policy. She reassured me that if the mom or baby was in distress, they would transport. After twenty-five hours of active labor with no pain medications, zero progression and uncontrollable tears, I demanded to be taken to the hospital. When I was admitted to the labor delivery unit, the midwife failed to inform the attending obstetrician I'd been in active labor for twenty-five hours! The ER staff was alarmed but immediately had a solution: an epidural and Pitocin. After forty-five hours of labor exhaustion, it was time to push. The physician put her panic aside, as staff became increasingly concerned for the safety of my daughter and I and helped to deliver my miracle daughter, Gabrielle. She was born a beautiful, healthy child thanks to a blend of modern medicine and the incredible knowledge I gained as a practicing Naturopathic Physician.

So why do I spend so much time and energy studying and practicing functional medicine? The answer is simple. I choose to be part of the healthcare system that brings forward "new thought." Whether it is natural or prescription medicines, nutrition, or mind-body medicine, I provide solutions for every patient. I love witnessing the healing power of quality, well researched nutritional supplements like Glutathione an incredible product to help with skin, immunity, inflammation, hormone balance, ADHD and Autism.

I also love serving as a thought leader that practices this new type of medicine. Ultimately, I have learned that when you do what you love, you cannot help but make a positive difference in the world and fulfill your unique purposes in life.

Karen Krysko

Intuitive/Medium, Energy Healer

Channeled-Wisdom

https://channeled-wisdom.com

https://www.linkedin.com/in/karenkrysko

https://www.instagram.com/karenkrysko_channeledwisdom

https://www.facebook.com/channeled.wisdom.1

Karen seemed like your regular little girl who grew up in Ontario Canada, but she secretly struggled with self-identity and confidence issues because she knew she was different.

She realized her "difference" was an intuitive nature that others couldn't feel/understand. As she honed in on her gifts, Karen's self-worth and confidence grew into magic. She now serves all those ready to reconnect with themselves by overcoming painful situations in their life that have caused blocks, setbacks, and physical illness.

What stands Karen apart from any other intuitive healer is that she finds the problems that are holding you back and gives you direct answers so you can move forward to live a joyful, limitless life filled with confidence, passion, purpose, and drive. Karen has appeared as a guest on radio stations and podcasts and has worked worldwide with celebrities, public figures, and healers.

Chapter 45

Going From Ordinary to Extraordinary

By Karen Krysko

What if you could shift your focus easily by taking a breath and quieting your mind, knowing that you would receive information that would transform lives? A superpower that holds such responsibility yet, could be looked upon with uncertainty.

If I could take you to a world that exists "behind my eyes," would you be willing to step up? How would you harness the voices, images and knowings alone? I never even asked myself if this intuitive nature of mine was real, I just knew it was and that it would have a purpose one day if I led a life with passion.

At a young age, I recognized that I was gifted with senses you may have only heard of in the movies. It was not looked upon as a real gift when I was younger, however, rather, voodoo, or witchy. I did not want this title nor to be judged, so I chose to take the path of least resistance and hide it, or so I thought.

I am sure most of you have been here before, living life yet not fully living. Your mind takes you in one direction, but your heart is telling you differently.

It takes courage to acknowledge these feelings and possibly decades to re-discover who you really are. With direct intention and action, change is inevitable.

Sometimes you need to take a step, not knowing what lies ahead; trusting that if you lead with intention, purpose and fear pushing vulnerability, it will take you to great heights.

After years of contemplation, I experienced the push. I left an unhealthy13-year marriage as a stay at home mom with three small kids. I prayed daily for things to work out. There was no correct formula, book, or list to follow. I trusted, believed and leaned into who I was and took the step. I was now raising and providing for my kids while starting a business and never looked back.

I believe everyone should pursue their passion in life. Discover your purpose, be self-aware, spend money on meaningful things, live with compassion and find a way to give back.

Here's how I went from deficient to free of resistance:

1. Follow your gut. It's one thing to know it, it's another to let it guide you.

2. Trust the process and lean in wholeheartedly.

3. Live each day with intention and only do things that align with your vision

When you believe in yourself and the choices you make, your confidence and worth grow automatically. Naturally, your mind intentionally aligns with trusting what comes your way, allowing for new opportunities and possibilities to flow. It takes patience, but you will get there. When you discover your *"why"* you are ***prepared*** in life for whatever comes. It's that preparedness that propels you to the extraordinary.

I didn't know I would do it, but I did it anyway. I choose to live life with purpose and passion focusing on the ordinary moments which have turned into extraordinary experiences.

Kathryn Whittington

Commissioner

Ashtabula County

http://www.ashtabulacounty.us/220/Commissioners

https://m.facebook.com/votekathrynw/?ref=bookmarks

Kathryn Whittington was elected to serve on the Ashtabula County Board of Commissioners on January 3, 2017 for a four (4) year term of office. Commissioner Whittington was re-elected to serve an additional four (4) year term of office to begin on January 3, 2021.

Kathryn has been working diligently since elected on the drug epidemic locally, statewide and nationally. She has created an initiative, Rural America, and spoken across the country on the prevention efforts and successes of Ashtabula County. Kathryn supports law enforcement and was instrumental in the creation of the new Crime Enforcement Agency of Ashtabula County (CEAAC), a drug task force that serves Ashtabula County.

Kathryn was previously employed with Ashtabula County Children Services, serving the children and families of Ashtabula County for 15 years and has over 25 years of experience working with families and communities. She was formerly the Community Service Coordinator for Ashtabula County Children Services Board.

Kathryn currently serves on various Health & Human Services Committees as well as Justice & Public Safety Committees through the County Commissioners Association of Ohio and the National Associations of Counties.

Kathryn is a West Geauga High School graduate and has an Associate's Degree in Business Administration Management and a Bachelor's Degree in General Business Administration.

Chapter 46

A Victims Journey to Victory

By Kathryn Whittington

Being an elected County Commissioner was not my lifelong dream. My dream was to make a difference. Find a way to serve. Work with children and families. Be the voice for those who needed to be heard.

What I thought was my life story has is in reality been a life journey of servitude. God has shown me the different paths of servitude and how life has many stories and chapters that create the journey.

Though my journey of servitude started at a young age, this chapter begins on October 9, 2013 when the back doors of my house were kicked in and it was burglarized by individuals addicted to drugs. We had just finished building the house and I had only been in the home 4 months. Boxes unpacked made the burglary easy. I had labeled all the boxes. Feeling victimized, I searched for suspects and answers. Every moment was consumed by this crime. I wanted justice.

Following the burglary, I contacted my county commissioner. My community had drug problems and jail issues. I was in the office for 5 minutes before being told my remarks and concerns were not accurate. I left the office and thought to myself, wow this is not how government should address a genuine concern of a constituent. This was the catalyst that led me to run for County Commissioner.

I was currently employed at Children Services, but being a classified employee, I could not run for a partisan office. I submitted my resignation.

As a candidate for office, I had zero political experience. I was referred to as a second or third-tier candidate. I was sure this wasn't good, I probably wanted to be a first-tier candidate. I won my first election and my re-election. I am now serving my second term as one the Ashtabula County Commissioners.

As a commissioner I have focused my energy into making a difference for the residents. I have focused on the jail issue, the drug epidemic and getting my community healthy and working again. I have been the voice bringing concerns to state and federal legislators.

Little did I know, another chapter was about to start. I received the call that no parent wants. Your son has overdosed and has been sent to the local addiction treatment facility. Unfortunately, his story hasn't changed yet. I received custody of 3 of his children in 2020. They have been with me since 2018. Being an elected official and juggling a family is a challenge.

When elected, I didn't want to be the commissioner whose role was already defined. I needed to define how that role would look like. I have encompassed my passion for serving and defined my role accordingly. I have instituted many successful programs, I was part of the creation of our drug task force, awarded grant funds and achieved advocacy locally, statewide and federally.

The way you can make a difference in your life, your community, or your servitude is by volunteering your time, participating in community collaboratives, organizing fund raisers and partnering with agencies, schools, businesses and local government to help creative initiatives to provide necessary resources to children and families.

I am not a victim in my personal or my professional life and you do not have to be either. I am victorious!

Maricela DeMarco

CERTIFIED MINDSET, SPIRITUAL COACH & REIKI
PRACTITIONER

Virtual Creative Solutions and Three Angels

https://www.threeangels.shop

https://virtualcreativesolutions.com

https://www.linkedin.com/in/maricela-demarco-3080b383

https://www.instagram.com/maricela_demarco

https://www.facebook.com/maricela.marindemarco

Maricela DeMarco is an entrepreneur and a self-made businesswoman, she is a certified mindset and transformational coach, reiki practitioner and a professional Virtual Assistant. She loves meditation, self-development and all practices of Self-Care. She shares with the world her personal experience on how she navigated, survived and Thrived through grief. She resides in Nevada with her husband and daughters, and when she is not working on her self-development you can find her in her social media supporting and inspiring others.

She dedicates this book to her daughters Crystal Saucedo, Samantha DeMarco and in loving memory of her daughter Valerie Saucedo-Romero. If you like to learn more about her, please connect with her via FB and Instagram.

Chapter 47

Thriving During Grief

By Maricela Demarco

You know those moments where the world seems to crack open and you never see things the same way ever again?

I've experienced many moments like those throughout my lifetime, but none of them compare to the immense and tremendous loss of my firstborn daughter Valerie, the death of my beautiful daughter has been the most heartbreaking, chest crushing, gut wrenching, breath stealing and most difficult challenge I had to overcome.

Losing a child of any age is an indescribable journey of survival, coping with their absence brings up every emotion imaginable. There are no rules for grieving and time becomes insignificant in so many ways, at least this has been my personal experience. I'm not going to lie to you. It will never become easy. The sorrow of losing your son or daughter will never lessen.

What I can tell you is that it will change. If you refuse to give up, you will find life again, in your own time, you will learn to survive and live around the pain and emptiness. It will not always be as suffocating and debilitating as it is right now. If you choose to take the steps to healing your inner self, you will find joy once again.

Through my experience I've learned that a grieving parent's worst nightmare is for our children's lives to be forgotten.

We want them to be remembered, we want everyone that met them to remember that they LIVED and they brought so much love and joy into this world, that they were loved so deeply.

How did I find a way to navigate through the deepest sorrow of my life?

I voted to take my time, I didn't rush the process, I allowed myself to sit in the emptiness and gave grief time to UNFOLD. I allowed myself to be under construction, I dedicated most of my time to REALLY explore self-love, self-care, including prayer, meditation, reiki, sound vibrational healing, yoga, this is how "Three Angels Shop" was born.

I have met so many parents walking this same unbearable journey and most of them want this to be over as if we have a time limit to grieve and move on. I often tell those parents there is no limit or expiration date to grieving, grieving is a POWERFUL emotion as powerful as LOVE is, there is nothing wrong with Love so there shouldn't be anything wrong with grieving and honoring the precious memory of our beloved children.

How you choose to honor your son or daughter is your choice.

I choose to honor my daughter Valerie by learning how to let go of any blame, by learning to smile and laugh again, by choosing to speak her name and tell stories of her life, by choosing to share my journey to healing, by choosing to CREATE my dream job this is how "Virtual Creative solutions" was born. For I read not long ago that there is no such thing as finding your dream job, but you can create it.

In loving Memory of Valerie Saucedo-Romero

Your Mommah Bear Maricela DeMarco

Mary Vila

Founder and Principal Coach

Mary Vila Coaching and Consulting

https://www.linkedin.com/in/maryvila

https://www.facebook.com/mary.vila.88

Mary Vila is a leadership coach and trainer with a passion for helping leaders uncover or rediscover their purpose, tap into their strengths and unblock what is stopping them from fully realizing their potential and living their best life. Mary has extensive experience leading global teams in startups, mid-sized and large organizations. She draws upon her own learning experiences, including the more painful ones, in her coaching and leadership development work.

Mary's sweet spot is working with highly motivated "critical middle" leaders – those in key mid-management roles who rise quickly and are accountable for the important work of carrying out their organizations mission. If their development as leaders is shortchanged or veers off track, it can have far-reaching consequences for them and the teams they lead. Without the right support, they can be left overwhelmed, overworked, and looking for a way out instead of a way up.

Using a series of powerful questions, assessments and other tools, Mary takes leaders on a journey of self-reflection and self-affirmation to find the answers within themselves, arming them with tools and resources to utilize now and to equip them for success as they progress in their careers.

Mary is an ICF certified leadership coach trained in a variety of assessments including Myers-Briggs, DISC, the Energy Leadership Index (ELI), and the Emotional Quotient Inventory (EQ-I2.0). She earned her undergraduate degree in Psychology from LaSalle University and completely graduate coursework in Organizational Dynamics at the University of Pennsylvania. She has certifications in Strategic Leadership from Cornell University and in Positive Psychology from Penn.

Chapter 48

Coming Full Circle

By Mary Vila

Looking back with the wisdom that comes from experience and the passage of time, I began my career with no clear idea about what I wanted to do with my life. I was fascinated by psychology and had a vague notion that pursuing that path would lead me into a purposeful career, one in which I could help to make the world a better place. I initially chose the field of child psychology, but a hospital internship working with troubled teens taught me that I was far too emotionally attached to be effective in that setting.

Motivated to use my psychology background in an environment that would be less emotionally draining, I stumbled upon a career in Human Resources. Again, in hindsight, I clearly didn't understand the nuances of the business world! My first job was as a compensation analyst and I hated every minute of it. Although I stayed in the job to satisfy my need for purpose, I volunteered (and slept) in a homeless women's shelter in Philadelphia every week for a few years. In listening to these women's stories, I was struck by the fact that many of them had started life very much as I had. Difficult circumstances, poor choices, financial instability or other issues had left them rudderless and lost in the system. This experience fueled me with a new resolve to be a success in my career. It also guided me to realize that I wanted to help others do the same.

Soon after, I was offered the opportunity to create and run a development program for high potential leaders. Despite my very limited experience, I was entrusted with hiring, developing, training, and coaching early in career professionals to prepare them for senior management roles. I was in truth, petrified at first by the level of responsibility the role entailed. Still, I dove in headfirst, learning everything I could about leadership development.

I learned that to develop great leaders, I needed to be a strong leader myself and that this meant taking risks, learning from mistakes and garnering support from others. In addition to providing a formidable foundation for my career, this experience instilled within me a powerful desire to continue my personal growth as a leader so that I could grow other leaders along the way.

Since that early experience, I have held senior leadership positions in various organizations, from start-ups to divestitures. At points throughout my journey, I have felt overwhelmed, burned out and ill-prepared. Still, during times of uncertainty including job loss, I have also received the greatest gifts. I have come to appreciate the value of pausing, reflecting and checking in with myself. These moments have given me time to recharge, learn new skills and reassess my plan where am I, what have I learned and how can I take this experience forward to the next challenge?

After leaving the corporate world in late 2020, I am coming full circle by again serving as a leadership coach. I am exhilarated to once again focus on helping talented people develop into the amazing leaders they are meant to be. Above all, I am grateful for the opportunity to have yet another shot at satisfying my need for purpose.

Michele Saunders

Founder/Mindset Coach

Thrive365

https://www.thrive365coach.com

https://www.linkedin.com/in/michele-saunders

https://www.instagram.com/michsaunders2

https://www.facebook.com/thrive365coach

https://www.facebook.com/michele.r.saunders

Michele is a Mindset Coach who specializes in helping women after a career break find their confidence, purpose, and discover their heartfelt passion to powerfully create their next chapter. Michele spent 10 years in corporate training and development facilitating the growth of employees at various worldwide firms by fostering communication and management skills. After taking many years away from her career to spend time raising her children, Michele returned to work and pursued a career in coaching.

She founded Thrive365 in June 2019 and is now looking to help other women find their own power and self-belief with her program "Reignite Now!". Michele loves exploring how one's mindset can help one overcome obstacles in life.

Michele earned a BA in History from Trinity College, Hartford, CT; an MSW from The Silver School of Social Work, NYU; and a professional certification in coaching from The Institute for Professional Excellence in Coaching (iPEC).

Chapter 49

Practicing Courage

By Michele Saunders

I was raised in a close-knit family of five in a charming, college town called Princeton, NJ. I always felt safe and happy, surrounded by family, friends and neighbors. I was blessed with a very normal life.

At 11, when my father suddenly died from cardiac arrest, my world abruptly changed and I began my journey of practicing courage. At that young age, I immediately felt the need to push forward, live as "normal" a life as possible and bravely face each new day. This mindset helped me navigate growing up during my formative years. I was aware of the change and heartache, but did not allow it to stagnate me.

As a young adult, while I watched my sister battle cancer, I again knew I had to remain strong and find my courage. I wanted to be there for her each step of the way. When she passed at 37, I summoned my courage to again begin my grieving and healing.

Due to these two major losses, I worried about the "other shoe dropping." What could happen next? Was this a pattern that would be repeated? It definitely was frightening.

Worrying did not help me. Rather, it skewed my perspective and prevented me from handling stress in a way that felt productive. I found that what did support me was believing in myself, in my strength and in my philosophy that life is to be embraced and cherished. Through this lens, I found the courage I needed to fully enjoy life without guilt, fear or doubt. I have seen how when courage is your ally, you can handle any obstacle.

No matter what we face that brings insecurity or fear, mustering the courage to ride life's ups and downs will help. Regardless of how unknown the waters, courage has helped me dip my toes into new beginnings and see the beauty of possibility.

Overall, my philosophy around courage centers on remaining present, enjoying life to the fullest, appreciating blessings and braving new territories.

How can *you* manifest a mindset of embracing courage?

I offer these suggestions:

- Recognize that to have courage does not mean you don't feel fearful, fear can be embraced rather than ignored.

- Learn to trust your intuition. Your own strength and inner wisdom will carry you forward.

- Actively collect evidence from successful experiences to affirm your own abilities. With every strong decision and action, you build your courage muscle.

- Adopt a belief that opportunity and possibility abound. There is no limit to your potential.

These tips have guided me for years. Beginning with my early childhood, to creating my own business at 57 years old, finding courage has always proven to be my "go to." The mindset of embracing the here and now and excitedly looking forward, has been more rewarding than holding myself back, hiding behind fear and limiting myself. In my role as a Mindset Coach, I am honored to help others discover their own courage as well.

Michele Saunders

Carolyn Rainwater

Author, Speaker, Lecturer, Professional Counselor

Rainwater Counseling, LLC

https://www.rainwatercounseling.net

https://www.linkedin.com/in/carolynrainwater

https://www.instagram.com/carolyn._rainwater

https://www.facebook.com/Rainwater-Counseling-LLC-102951504946417

https://www.facebook.com/carolyn.rainwater.50

Author, Speaker, Lecturer, Professional Counselor and Master's Level Addiction Counselor, Carolyn Rainwater, MA., LPC, LMAC, loves to assist others in healing, defining goals, and reaching their heartfelt life dreams and purposeful callings. She is an artist, and enjoys music production as she is thankful for her faith and family.

Carolyn has completed Post Graduate work in Autism Education and Military Resiliency, and a graduate of Valley Hope Counselor Training Program. Carolyn is a Certified Faith Based Counselor with the Faith Based Counselor Training Institute and holds a MA in Professional Counseling, BA in Business and Human Relations, and AS in Science, emphasis Addictions. Member of the American Association of Christian Counselors.

Chapter 50

Two Dreams

By Carolyn Rainwater

I forgot to dream. As a child, I penned, "A light lingers on when times are low, love is gone, hope wants to grow". I grew up in a home with a father plagued with alcoholism and brother that eventually, lost the battle to lifelong addiction. I needed this message of hope. A loss of hope feels like heaviness on the heart. God promises to open up our understanding so that we can know and experience the hope within his calling, Ephesians 1: 18-23 (NIV).

Recently, in a dream, I saw a message written in a yearbook to a particularly famous, extremely successful person. A thought-out vision, with a positive outlook and kind encouragement was cast for the future. The owner of the book read it and believed it! I can imagine, that some of you have experienced the same kind of messages when passing various milestones in your own lives. I suppose you read the messages and believed them at the time. Perhaps, you took these old-fashioned blogs, as a life plan, even in parts and lived them out. Others, read theirs too, but they did not believe dreams were really possible. Furthermore, some did not write even a wish for themselves. Hope for them, appeared lost.

In another dream, I heard the aspirations of young people in China. They stood in a place that looked like a cave, dark but filled with the light of their hopes. Young men and women somehow believed they could accomplish their dreams where careers were mandated to them from the collective society in which they lived. I heard their longings to become a journalist, an architect, teacher, business owner, scientist and other various careers. I felt sad for them because it seemed their path was chosen for them by powers greater than self.

In free nations, dreams thought, or written down can become a reality in life. Hopes become real and dreams suffer not. Western society shouts, be all that you can be, but seldom is there a kind of mentorship that truly touches the heart of a dreamer to recognize their extreme potential. On the other hand, collective societies sometimes accomplish great dreams at the expense of the individual. Wherever you live, perhaps the answer is not only found in your own dreams, but in hope holding and faith that God has a specific plan within the calling. I pray you find this place.

Fear mandates silence to speak and live the vision of our lives, but faith in God is the power and real living force that can launch destiny. God brings people together miles apart in distance or ideology. Through faith and prayerful action, one can write the yearbook message, live life with dreams and hope beyond current circumstances. I love to aspire others to realize their worth and begin to dare to dream. Hope is forged in the suffering. Beyond this expectation, when mixed with faith and prayers, we are led to our destiny.

Sonia Petkewich

Founder, Community Leader & CEO

Taurean Consulting Group, Catalyst Collaborative Mastermind

www.taureanconsulting.net

www.catalyst.vegas

https://www.linkedin.com/in/soniathecatalyst

https://www.facebook.com/sonia.petkewich

As the owner and CEO of Taurean Consulting Group — a 100 percent woman-owned IT staffing and project solutions company in Las Vegas — Sonia Petkewich believes relationship building is the key to professional success.

With a personal motto of "leaving things better than she found them," Sonia is always looking for possibilities and solutions for clients and job candidates. With over 20 years in the staffing industry, she brings a wealth of experience to the Taurean team.

In addition to owning and operating a top recruiting company, Sonia is also a community leader of the Catalyst Collaborative Mastermind Group, which acts as Board of Directors for its members. After purchasing Taurean in 2015, Sonia was able to catapult it to a $5 million business in three years with the support of Catalyst.

In addition to her work with Catalyst, Sonia is also Interim President of the Southern Nevada chapter of the National Association of Women Business Owners (NAWBO) and LV Techies. Along with her passion for all things Las Vegas, Sonia also supports the causes of Women Empowerment, Girls in Tech, and ITWorks, and enjoys mentoring and coaching other women with small businesses to help them achieve results.

In her free time, Sonia loves experiencing new adventures with her husband of 18 years, Ben, and their three children, ages 10, 13 and 15, including many Saturdays spent on the soccer field and Sundays watching the Las Vegas Aviator, Las Vegas Raiders and Vegas Golden Knights.

Chapter 51

Mastermind Your Business to Success

By Sonia Petkewich

As the saying goes, "if you want to make more money, give more money away." I have found another universal truth "if you want to do work you love, help others do work they love."

I've been in the recruiting business over 20 years and the best part about the job comes after we place a candidate in a job, we feel is a great fit. Then, maybe a month later, or even again a year later, we check back in and hear the magic words all recruiters love to hear, "thank you for helping me find the job of my dreams." Results like that make my work so rewarding.

Helping others find work they love has only led to more opportunities for me to do work I love. So much so, that now I've been able to take everything to the next level. Recruiting remains my core "helping others" business. Coaching has become my "giving back" business.

When I started my recruiting business, I was fortunate enough to have people around me who believed in me, encouraged me and kept me motivated. Especially during the down times, when success wasn't the clear outcome. These people gave me the support I needed to keep going when things got tough. I wanted to give that sense of support and community to other business owners. The best way I found to do that was to build a mastermind community.

A business-oriented mastermind is a group of business owners who share a growth mindset and they exist for the purpose of helping each other grow and develop both professionally and personally. Members of a mastermind group are purposefully and regularly surrounding themselves with other people who are committed to developing themselves and their businesses. It is like having a trusted group to call you on your BS, a guide that reminds you of what you have declared as your truth, what you say is important to you.

I launched the mastermind to support and help other business owners when I saw a need in my community. I did it for free, to create a tribe and a space for business owners to come together and support each other through a traumatic and very difficult year for small businesses. Now it continues and has become a profitable enterprise.

I have been so fortunate to help other business owners by mentoring and guiding them through the ups and downs of entrepreneurship. Three benefits of joining a mastermind are: like-minded people, focused accountability and opportunity to work on your business instead of in your business.

My true love for work in this space manifests when the light bulb lights and a business owner sees herself as capable. All things become possible and the story that did not serve her, the one that's been holding her back, that she's been telling herself for years, finally stops running on a loop. I get to witness that firsthand. It's inspiring. Now it's my most favorite and most fulfilling work to do.